Invitation to MANAGEMENT

INVITATION SERIES

Invitation to Archaeology	Philip Rahtz
Invitation to Astronomy	Jacqueline and Simon Mitton
Invitation to Economics	David Whynes
Invitation to Engineering	Eric Laithwaite
Invitation to Industrial Relations	Tom Keenoy
Invitation to Linguistics	Richard Hudson
Invitation to Philosophy	Martin Hollis
Invitation to Politics	Michael Laver
Invitation to Social Work	Bill Jordan
Invitation to Statistics	Gavin Kennedy

Other titles in preparation

Invitation to Anthropology	Maurice Bloch
Invitation to Mathematics	John Bowers
Invitation to Medicine	Douglas Black
Invitation to Nursing	June Clark
Invitation to Psychology	Philip Johnson-Laird
Invitation to Teaching	Trevor Kerry

Invitation to MANAGEMENT

Peter Lawrence

BASIL BLACKWELL

First published in 1986

Basil Blackwell Ltd
108 Cowley Road, Oxford OX4 1JF, UK

Basil Blackwell Inc.
432 Park Avenue South, Suite 1505,
New York, NY 10016, USA

British Library Cataloguing in Publication Data
Lawrence, P.A.
Invitation to management.—(Invitation series)
1. Management
I. Title
658 HD31

ISBN 0–631–14683–0
ISBN 0–631–14684–9 Pbk

Library of Congress Cataloging in Publication Data
Lawrence, Peter (Peter A.)
Invitation to management.
(Invitation series)
Bibliography: p.
Includes index.
1. Executive ability. I. Title. II. Series.

HD38.2.L38 1986 658.4 85–20049
ISBN 0–631–14683–0
ISBN 0–631–14684–9 (pbk.)

Typeset by Oxford Publishing Services, Oxford
Printed and Bound in Great Britain by
T.J. Press (Padstow) Ltd, Padstow, Cornwall

For Patricia Ann Lawrence

Contents

Acknowledgements

My main debt is to the managers at many levels in a variety of companies, in several countries, but especially in my native Britain, who have helped me with my research and talked to me about their jobs. Anyone who tries to write a book about management as a real-life activity can only get to it in this way, and I am grateful to have had the chance.

Four of my former students at the University of Loughborough wrote undergraduate dissertations which I have used to substantiate various themes in this book. In this connection I would like to thank Joanna Dunn, Karen McMahon, John Mansfield and Tyrone Smith. I have also taken some of the ideas on corporate culture from another former student, Julian Barrowcliffe.

My friend Alan Bryman at Loughborough University gave me invaluable help with the intellectual design of the last two chapters, and both he and John Morris at the Manchester Business School got me reading the right things at a critical time.

I would like to thank several of the secretaries in the Management Studies Department at the University of Loughborough including Marion Aitkenhead, Rosemary Babington, Olivia Fergus, Kathleen Gibson and Aeron Hall.

Responsibility for the text and interpretation naturally rests with me.

1

Knowledge or Activity

It may be one of the ironies of American history that George Washington was really a jerk. Certainly he did not enjoy in life, and especially in the last ten years of his life, the unequivocal esteem granted by posterity.

In life Washington was one of the most vilified of American presidents and his political career one of the most controversial. The influential Philadelphia newspaper *Aurora* in 1796 went as far as to declare: 'If ever a nation was debauched by a man, the American nation has been by Washington.' A year later when Washington left office the *Aurora* noted: 'If ever there was a period for rejoicing, it is this moment.'

Yet to say he was rehabilitated after death would be an understatement. He was eulogised, glorified, and mystified. The production of uncritical and hagiographic biographies became a national industry. Shortage of factual information, especially about Washington's early life, facilitated jolly good stories that were not likely to be challenged (who, after all, could prove that he had not chopped down a cherry tree in the seclusion of the paternal garden). Washington also achieved an immense posthumous popularity as a subject of public orations. The record here is no doubt held by Edward Everett who delivered (the same!) 2-hour oration 129 times in a 4-year period. Everett's characterisation of (the young) Washington will give the tenor:

> The character of Washington, twenty-four years of age, a model of manly strength and beauty, perfect in all the qualities and accomplishments of the gentleman and the soldier, but wise and thoughtful

beyond his years, inspiring at the outset of his career that love and confidence which are usually earned only by a life of service.[1]

This transition raises an interesting question. How have we progressed from 'debaucher of a nation' to 'perfect in all the qualities . . .'?

It is argued by Daniel Boorstin, a leading cultural historian of the USA, that precisely because nineteenth-century America was young, new, and insecure it had a desperate need to create idols, symbols, and a depth of history. The glorification of George Washington was part of a general movement of parodoxically insecure national assertiveness.

Something similar happened to management. When it was young, insecure, and largely American it invented too many idols, made too many claims. The result is that there is confusion about the nature of management. Is it an activity, or a subject, and if it seems to be both how do they relate? And if management is a subject (as well) what kind of a subject; one subject, or many subjects? And where is management? Is it all levels in hierarchic organisations or only in the upper levels; is it peculiar to business and manufacturing organisations, or common to all formal organisations whatever their purpose? This first chapter will try to sort out some of these questions.

A WORKING DEFINITION

Management is usually defined as getting things done with or through other people. It involves making decisions about objectives and means to achieve the ends set and more frequently making decisions to solve lots of problems that will otherwise frustrate the achievement of these objectives. Management is about planning and organising to get things done, and especially about coordinating, about bringing together, reconciling and integrating various activities or parts of the task that all contribute to the whole. It is also about controlling or making sure things are going according to plan, that objectives are being realised, and often a lot of thought and energy goes into generating information that will facilitate this control. The organisation in which this is all happening is made up of people, not mechanical parts, so that relations between people, communicating and maintaining commitment are all important.

What we have just done is to define management as an activity, and this is not difficult or even particularly controversial. What is more difficult is distinguishing between management as an activity, a subject, and an idea. Let us take the idea next.

CONSCIOUSNESS CREATES REALITY

The paradox is that management acts were undoubtedly performed before people were conscious of management, or put a name to it. Building the pyramids, for instance, involved some planning and organising, and marshalling of human resources; or again Napoleon must have done a bit of communicating and motivating when he took his enormous army to Moscow in 1812.[2] Yet the idea of management, consciousness of it as a distinctive and distinguishable activity only really emerged in the USA in the nineteenth century. This consciousness was induced by quite exceptional conditions. From the time the War of Independence against the British was ended in 1783 till the last unclaimed land was distributed at Fort Sill, Oklahoma in 1890, the Americans 'filled in' a continent. It is a story of too much space, too few people, too many opportunities and not enough skill to go round. The thing that was most needed and therefore most celebrated was organising ability. And of course there was never quite enough of it to go round, which gave rise to the accompanying American idea that it must be possible to train for it.

It is usual to cite the financing and constructing of the American railroads as the activity which called forth 'management' in its modern form, but the railroads were the apotheosis rather than the inspiration. At an earlier stage quite critical activities for a developing but sparsely settled country put a premium on organisation.

Take the fur trade. In Canada nicely trained Indians trapped furry animals and brought them to the white-man's trader settlements. But the American Indians were more migratory and less obliging so white settlers themselves conducted the fur trade. They went out and trapped animals, but more important they got the skins to a variety of unsettled pick-up points manned according to a schedule. This was not easy in the age before micros, telex, and quartz watches: it took some organising.

Or again there were the caravans, the assemblies of people and waggons crossing first the Appalachians and later the Prairies and Rockies in the colonising drives to the west and south. These were not organised by any public authority, were not even government sponsored: people went on them because they wanted to and thought they would be happier, richer, or freer at journey's end than at the starting point. So these voyaging groups elected caravan captains to run the show, made up their own rules, regulated their communal affairs for months on end, and where necessary set up their own field courts martial.

Another imperative need for regulation was in the area of land claims, where people were occupying land too quickly and too far away from the seat of federal government. Again self-organisation arose in the form of elected claim clubs which rationalised nascent patterns of land occupation and inhibited claim jumping.

Side by side with these particular challenges to organisational ability there is something more general happening. Settling a new area is not the end of desire but its beginning. Those who settle want to attract others, want the settlement to grow, to have services and amenities, to have status and importance and to be the best place around and not play second fiddle to the township up the road. In other words these settlements are striving, growing, competing. This leads to what Daniel Boorstin calls 'boosting'.[3] Small townships would set up newspapers long before there was a population to sustain the paper's circulation, seeing this as a way to boost population. They would rush to build hotels because a town with a hotel is not a one-horse town any more. High schools and even more universities serve the same end.

There is a strong element of rivalry in all this. Townships entered into local civil wars with each other over the competition to be designated county seat (local administrative centre). When the railroads were planned and built there was intense competition to have the line pass through your town and not the neighbouring one and these rivalries explain some of the delay in railroad construction as well as some of the zig-zag tracks.

In short, a whole series of needs, specific and general, put a premium on organising skills especially when crossed with versatility. The ideal settler could pass from caravan captain to claim-club chairman, run a newspaper, lobby the county seat, help found a university, and pull strings to get the railroad over their way. It is all about getting things done through people, with the emphasis on the skill and process rather than on the content of particular assignments. This is how the idea of management is born.

Indeed it is possible to give the argument a further twist and say that the emerging consciousness of management is also a response to American heterogeneity. While the people have different backgrounds, often different national origins, they are alike, even unified, by their need for organising talent and generous recognition of its appearance.

If, of course, management is both identifiable and desirable the next step is to organise its inculcation. In the USA this turned out to be a short step.

CAN YOU TEACH IT?

As we approach the end of the century the United Kingdom sports three business schools, the first of them, the London Business School, founded in 1965.[4] In the USA there are several hundred, and the first, Wharton at Philadelphia, was founded in 1881 (just after we British had ended the purchase of army commissions!). This contrast is a testimony to the American conviction that management is not only 'a good thing' but also 'a teachable thing'. Is this right?

It has become almost fashionable to say that management cannot be taught, or more properly that managers cannot be produced by teaching. Certainly plenty of British companies run the line that management training is their preserve, not that of the higher-education system. 'We like to grow our own timber,' and 'We know what our managers need to know,' say representatives of these companies. The view that managers cannot be produced by the educational system rests on two premises.

The first is the implicit view that management is a somewhat intangible activity, therefore a talent for it can only be developed through practical experience, on the job exposure. This idea can perhaps best be highlighted by a contrast. Management is not like, say, learning the morse code, which one can be taught in the classroom, and then those who have been taught can go away and do the job as radio operators.

The second argument is to say that even given practice and exposure, not everyone has it in them to become a manager. There is clearly an intelligence threshold, a need for some modicum of emotional stability and personal robustness, and for social and political skills. Do these two arguments stand up?

The paradox is that they are both plausible and casuistic. While they make sense intrinsically there is a certain sleight of hand in their application. The two arguments are marshalled as though management were the only job marked by personality prerequisites and a need to develop by doing. Yet the whole spectrum of more interesting and more demanding jobs is like this. Are there not personality prerequisites for the jobs of doctor, teacher, and army officer? Can one become an effective journalist, detective, or actor purely on the basis of what is learned in the academy? Yet these well-recognised limitations are not reasons to neglect or derogate the training given to the would-be entrant to such occupations.

Management as an occupation should be seen in the same way. Training will make the most of potential, experience will necessarily develop capacity, but a relevant education is the best start. But perhaps more can be made of this contention by looking at the nature of a management education and the gains it confers.

ELEMENTS OF A MANAGEMENT EDUCATION

If we take as a prototype an undergraduate course in management or business administration and ask in what senses it is a valid preparation for management work, the answers will be at several levels and be variously couched in terms of context, analysis and theory, specialisation, process, and pure description.

Context is important. We are not born with an understanding of the context in which business enterprise functions, and the ordinary process of growing up yields only a limited understanding of this context. To this end management courses invariably include a basic economics course which sets the scene, shows how national and international economies are put together, relations between economic forces, and the interconnection between government policy and management performance. The nature and operation of financial institutions – banks, discount houses, stockbrokers, the stock exchange, and so on – will be included, and today it is increasingly common to look at the institutions and processes of international capital markets, bond dealings, international lending and investment, foreign currency transactions and ways to evaluate performance of business enterprises owned in one country but located in another.

But context is not conceived in exclusively economic terms. Companies operate at least within a national legal context, and often within the laws of a variety of countries with whom they do business. This makes an understanding both of the principles of the system and the law on particular issues, for example contract, debt, liability, very desirable. Or again, business enterprises employ people and many manufacturing establishments employ on a large scale, so that what is usually called the system of industrial relations is a relevant part of the overall context. In Britain such courses tend to cover the history of unionism, the types of trade union and their internal organisation, and the extraordinarily complicated issue of trends in union membership. The way unions recruit, their representation in the work place, the rights afforded them by law, and above all the ways in which wage settlements are achieved are typically part of such industrial relations courses.

In short, context may be understood in a variety of ways from the very specific things at one end of the spectrum to an appreciation of general social trends at the other.

The boundaries between the things mentioned at the outset – context, theory, process, and so on – are not always clear cut. In particular an education in theory and analysis usually goes hand in hand with a study of management specialisms such as accountancy, marketing, operations research, and so on, but it may be helpful to continue the arguments separately. Many of these specialisms have a body and theory, develop typologies (sets of types for classificational purposes), and analyse phenomena in semi-abstract ways.

Take organisational behaviour which deals both with the behaviour of people within organisations (manufacturing companies, business organisations) and with the character of the organisations themselves. This subject has theories, postulating dynamic relationships between organisations and their environment, and theories relating organisational objectives, structure, and technology, together with theories of leadership, motivation, satisfaction, alienation, and communication as they relate to managers and workers.

Or the subject of marketing, for instance, propounds what is called product life-cycle theory, showing the developmental stages through which a product will pass over time, the sales strategies and likely outcomes at these various stages, and the sequential inevitability. The concept of the marketing mix, to take another marketing example, expresses the idea that goods or services are sold as a result of a variety of initiatives and arrangements (the mix). What is more this mix is itself variable from one sales situation to another. One element in the mix, promotional advertising, for instance, is particularly important in the sale of some consumer goods, such as soap powders, whereas the efforts of individual salesmen are more critical in the sale of many industrial goods, such as machine tools.

It is at the level of specialisation that management degree courses come into their own. If one takes the subjects taught then our headings of context and specialisation cover most of what is on offer, and specialist courses are most numerous. There is for the most part a nice fit between these specialist courses making up an overall management degree and particular areas of management work.

So that courses in marketing may lead to and are preparation for jobs in sales, market research, advertising, and distribution; courses in accountancy and financial management offer an understanding of work in costing, budgeting, financial control, performance measurement, and financial administration generally; courses in personnel, production management, and occasionally purchasing all have a corresponding function in industry. Then again there is the range of mathematical subjects which relate in some way to business. There is statistics which has a variety of specialist applications in industry, operations research which is the global name for the use of mathematics in business decisions and problem solving, mathematical modelling which is a way of formulating problems to allow a manipulation of the variables, and courses to do with the use of computers, programming, and using computers to generate systems information useful to managers for decision-making or control. All these maths and computer subjects correspond to areas of work in management, especially in what are called management services departments. People working in these use their maths-based skills and computer facilities to devise information and control systems for other managers or departments, and to solve particular problems on an *ad hoc* basis where the problem is susceptible to some kind of systematic processing.

These particular courses that are the mainstay of management courses serve a number of different if overlapping ends.

First, as said, these specialisms do correspond to particular areas of management work – marketing, finance and administration, management services, and so on – and thus are an important preparation for actually working in these functions later. Second, and more generally important, they provide understanding and insight into the rationale and operation of these areas of management work. One may never actually work in many of these specialisms but it is still important to know what they are all about, how they fit with each other and contribute to overall company achievement. Take a practical example: business graduates are not usually very keen to work in the production department; production has a bit of a 'cloth cap' image, and it is not a way to the top. Yet all the other specialist departments – sales, purchasing, finance, management services, all the technical departments – interact with production. So it matters to understand how production works, on what principles it is organised, what its constraints, problems, and perceptions are.

As suggested earlier the teaching of these specialist subjects is also the occasion and vehicle for much exposition of theory and analysis. Some of the specialisms actually embody the mastery of specific techniques as well. This is most obviously true on the finance and quantitative analysis side. Thus one actually learns how to do balance sheets and cash-flow forecasts, and how to interpret profit and loss statements and write computer programmes, how to do basic market research, and how to approach product costing.

The case against the plethora of specialist courses making up the typical management degree, and students are quick to spot it, is that they tend not to leave very much time for management itself! The specialisms seem overrepresented, students find they know a lot about the particular but less about the general, the overview of how it is all put together is sometimes neglected, it is an education in the parts rather than the whole.

This brings us to what I called process at the start of this section. It represents the attempt to say something meaningful about management as a whole, rather than a study of its specialisms. The essence of management process courses is that they tend to focus on things that are common to management jobs in general, such as communication, coordination, delegation, motivation, controlling, information gathering, and problem solving. The more sophisticated courses on management process tend to go further with an analysis of relations and situations. They confront such questions, that is, as how do we make authority effective, how do we handle conflict, how do we obtain cooperation from people over whom we have no authority but upon whom we depend, and so on.

When management began as a subject it tended to be the general that was emphasised. Usually in the form of principles of management, exhortatory propositions about authority, responsibility, coordination, and morale. With the subsequent explosion of knowledge concerning contributory specialisms the centre of gravity of management degrees has shifted away from the general, except perhaps for courses on corporate strategy or business policy, courses, that is, about what companies need to do to keep on winning in a changing environment. The time is probably ripe for a movement of the pendulum back towards the general.

Finally, as a dimension of management courses, there is description. There is usually an element of description, of saying what it is like in the world of business and industry, in most courses, and this is necessarily so in the undergraduate context where the student has at least a provisional commitment to working in industry but has not worked there yet, and therefore needs some pure descriptive accounts of the way it is. Having said this, the descriptive element is usually no more than a part, and usually an introductory part, of various courses. That is probably a pity. It may well be that one of the most helpful things one can do for management undergraduates is to give them, quite systematically, a 'warts and all' picture of what industry is like. When I have asked students, who are returning to the university to complete their degree course after a year out in industry, what has surprised them most, the response tends to be in terms of counter-naivety: they speak of the conflicts, inefficiencies, rule-breaking, politics, and often of the things you do to get the job done that are not actually prescribed.

STOCKTAKING

Management is an idea, an activity, and a subject. As an activity, organising people and resources to get things done, it has always been with us though the volume of management activity has increased over historic time (from the building of the Pyramids to the divisionalisation of General Motors).

America after the War of Independence had an acute need for organisational talent, a practical social need for organisers, managers, setters-up, and fixers. Consciousness of the need led to its articulation, to a formulation and even a celebration of management. Management as an idea was 'made in USA'.

For the idea to serve the need, in the American case, a need that gently transmutes from organising in sparsely settled areas to running major industrial and commercial undertakings, management has to be seen as teachable and be taught in fact: management as a subject is born. Again it is the USA which leads in the establishment of business schools, in making management education a major concern of the higher education system.

The idea that management can be taught has not gone unchallenged, especially outside the USA. The twin arguments marshalled against it are the manager's need for practice and personality. The counter objection, and it is a major one, is that this applies generally to interesting and demanding jobs and there is no good reason to pick out management and run the argument selectively; education has the same role in developing managers as it does in creating barristers, bishops, and brigadiers.

At the same time it is important to see what gains are conferred by management education, what it can and cannot do. To an extent education can substitute for experience, because experience in the sense of the argument is a distillation not a time-activity block. Experience is what you know, not what happened to you. It is 'all in the mind', and some of it can be put there by educational processes. These processes have been presented in the last few pages in terms of context, theory, specialisation, process, and description, rather than in terms of a typical undergraduate syllabus, though with many references to such syllabi. It is arguable that in practice such courses veer more to the specialisms than to management process, and that opportunities for life-like description are missed, opportunities which might again substitute for experience. There is an acknowledged problem in management education in that it is easier to analyse management processes than to practise them.

In considering management as an idea it is important to go beyond identifying its origins and confront these other and related issues. In terms of the idea, who are the managers hierarchically? Who are they institutionally? Is the idea of management always and everywhere the same?

WHERE DOES MANAGEMENT START?

There is a sense in which the American management education lobby has overplayed its hand. Writers in this tradition make management sound so important and demanding that it comes over as the sport of supermen. And as we are not quite sure how to spot supermen then a safer guide is looking to people in the higher ranks in business organisations. Ergo, management is something that happens at the top. This implicit viewpoint is not so much wrong as incomplete, and it is worth looking at the opposite idea for a moment.

It is not an accident that the verb manage exists in everday speech as well as in management teaching. So that toddlers manage their teddy bears, housewives manage the weekly budget, people manage to fit in the gardening on Saturday afternoon, and most of the time students manage to pass exams. What we ought to be taking from this is the fact that managing is actually quite a common not to say homely activity.

If we put these two senses of managing together what emerges is that management is an element in many jobs, not the exclusive preserve of senior people in business organisations. This simple truth is probably obscured by the way we think about managers, in terms of authority and status trappings. A manager is someone who has twenty people reporting to him and an office on the top floor. But if we think of getting things done in conjunction with other people, not necessarily people under our command, then it is clear that management activity extends a long way down. What is more if one takes the planning and organising dimensions of management then the majority of jobs have a management input. Most industrial workers are making decisions about how and when to do things, planning small sequences, lining up resources both material and human. One has to look to very repetitive, short-cycle jobs in industry to find examples of work denuded of managing. In short managing is an element in most jobs. Management is thus not an absolute, but a continuum.

For the professionally qualified who enter industry the first job is not usually an explicitly managerial one. Such people are working primarily as accountants, marketing assistants, development scientists, production engineers or whatever, though this work will invariably involve organising and cooperating elements. Time, experience, and, for some, promotion, changes the picture to one in which the tasks are explicitly managerial. This transition may, and frequently is, depicted diagrammatically.

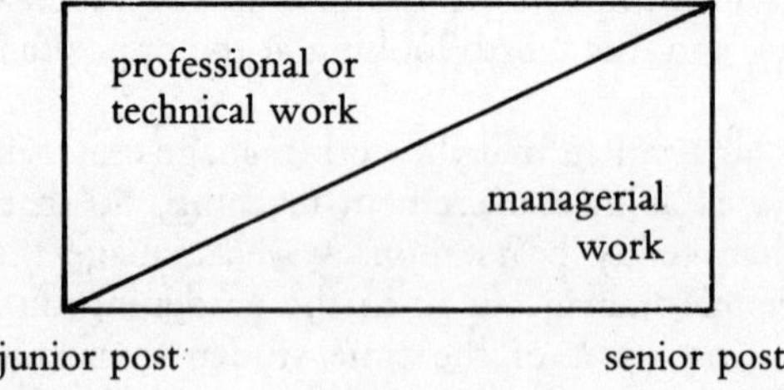

It is probably helpful to add a footnote to the impression given by the diagram. The transition is not simply one from more to less, there is some qualitative change in this as well in the sense of moving between different dimensions of managing. At the junior end it is planning and organising one's work, negotiating cooperation, and fitting it to the needs of others. At the senior end the emphasis has shifted to organising work for others and facilitating its accomplishment, setting their objectives, and fitting it to the needs of the company in ever more complicated ways. Managing is not monochrome, but a mix of related processes.

ALL THE WORLD IS A STAGE

For some time the idea has been growing that the countries of the world are becoming more and more alike. Or at least this is true for the Western countries, democratic, industrialised, and wealthy. Thus we are accustomed to see the same goods, the same advertising, the same companies, the same distributive arrangements, a scenario of industrialised uniformity with (the same) filling stations stretching from Kansas City to Corinth.

At perhaps a more serious level this same impression of homogeneity is fostered by management educators and consultants, whose precepts and insights are felt to be equally valid wherever industry is being managed.

The case for this view is a strong one, and it is logically compelling. Industrialism transcends frontiers, and has its own logic. Management is international and has its own principles and dynamic. It does not matter whether cars are being made in Detroit, Dagenham, Cologne, or Turin: car manufacture will present the same organisational and technical challenge. The world is a stage for performing the managing arts.

Notwithstanding the force of this argument it has to be said that management may be differently perceived in different countries. Again to understand this perceptual relativity one needs to emphasise the American origins. The consciousness of management, the idea of management, above all the conviction that management is something desirable which can be extrapolated, put on view, examined, and made the subject of synthesising generalisation, is American in inspiration. Not all societies have adopted this American conviction to the same degree, even if Britain in particular is a country much exposed to American influence.

To give substance to this charge that perceptions may vary it is worth looking at West Germany, a country every bit as industrialised and economically successful as the USA.[5] In Germany the idea of management developed later, the figure of the manager only slowly displacing that of the entrepreneur. The German language has never found an indigenous word for management but has simply taken over the American expression and its derivatives, on occasion joining them with German words to produce compound nouns (e.g. Managementkrankeit = management illness = stress; or Managementausbildung = management training).

The German view of management is more specialist and more technical. It is the specialist and technical content of jobs in industry which is emphasised rather than the general and managerialist aspect, and this is thoroughly reflected in management training. Courses in Germany tend to be all post-experience, that is, aimed at people who have completed full-time education and are already working in industry; these courses also tend to be specific as to the rank, needs, and work area of the particular managers they are aimed at. It is courses in production planning in the food-processing industry or training in export salesmanship in machine-tool manufacture, rather than courses on the principles of general administration or management process. German managers identify themselves in more functionally specific ways preferring labels such as a production engineer or salesman to the more general manager or executive.

Now Germany may well be a strong case of a country with differing assumptions about management, but something more general is at stake than German–American differences. This is that management is human and variable not divine and absolute. Management is a set of activities people perform and a subject which they teach; the idea of management is not inscribed on tablets of stone but exists in the minds of men. It is this variability which gives excitement to both the practice and analysis of management.

IN INDUSTRY OR IN ORGANISATIONS

When we talk about management do we refer to activites in industry or to similar organising and direction in the whole range of formal organisations including military organisations, the civil service, local government bodies, even hospitals and universities? There is no right or wrong answer, it can be argued either way.

The tendency has been to stress the similarities between industrial management and civil administration. Especially in the higher positions, it is claimed, there is a similarity in the prerequisites and constraints. Leadership, authority, policy review, and decision-making are common to both. The processes of communication, negotiation, and control are similar as between many types of formal organisation.

The subject of organisational behaviour referred to in discussing the elements of management education tends to reinforce the general view of similarity across various types of organisations. Indeed the essence of organisational behaviour (OB) is the characterisation of organisations *per se*, and of behaviour within them. This focus tends to be homogenising, to see patterns and parallels which transcend the boundaries between organisation types. OB is at its most exuberant in demonstrating that the local tennis club and a Nazi concentration camp have various elements of organisational structure and process in common.

I want to argue the reverse. That there are real differences between these 'managing jobs' in the different kinds of organisations, and this book is in consequence about managers and management in industry.

There are several reasons for feeling that management in industry is distinctive and deserves separate treatment. First industry aims to make a profit and this makes it qualitatively different from all other organisational types. It means there is always a certain duality and richness of objective in industry. Business organisations want to make a profit and often to grow and diversify as well. But profit making is not a transitive-verb activity. Companies do not in any literal sense make money (the mint does that). They make goods and provide services, and if people want to buy them, and the buying price exceeds the cost of provision, then the company makes money. So that the manufacturing and selling exercises are a means to the end of profit, and at the same time they are also the major activity. This duality makes business organisations fascinatingly different; creative and complex activities are endlessly reviewed in terms of profit performance and potential. So when companies are established they have this dual *raison d'être* of a technically viable product, service, or operation, at the same time assessed by cost and likely demand for profit potential.

Second it is only industry that has the full range of departments or functions – design and the various technical functions, purchasing, manufacturing, marketing, personnel, finance, and management services. The contrast with, say, a civil service department at this point is stark. The civil service department does not typically design anything (except policy), it does not make anything, sell anything, or earn anything. It is a general administrative entity engaging in a bit of personnel administration on the side. This range of functions found in the typical manufacturing company is interesting in several ways. They correspond to various courses of a management degree as was shown earlier. The nature of work in these different functions varies greatly, an idea which will be developed in chapter 3, so that for instance an export salesman in a textile firm has more in common with an export manager in a rival company than with, say, a home-territory salesman in his own company. What is more the way the company is put together in the sense of interconnections between the functions is both variable and critical. Much of the work of individual managers consists of trading, liaising, and negotiating with other functions.

Third the ethos of industry is sharply different from that of the civil service, and not only in the sense of the pursuit of profit although that is doubtless a mainspring. The values of the service are probity, procedural rectitude, impartiality, an ethic of service, the application of educated cleverness to policy evaluation. The ethos of industry differs in the emphasis placed on getting it right, not being in the right. It is about seeing and exploiting opportunities, sticking it together somehow, cutting corners, bluff, resourcefulness and making it happen. This is enough difference for a separate book.

Does this mean that the book will only benefit those intending to take a course or make a career in industrial management? No, it does not, because the part of the argument I have chosen not to emphasise, the organisational behaviour view of the commonalities, also has some validity, with the result that some of the processes treated here are relevant to managing in other organisations even if I have placed them in the context of profit-making companies.

But perhaps more important than this is the consideration that profit-making organisations are an important part of the landscape of all Western countries yet are typically not well understood by the outsiders (the majority of the citizenry). By giving an idea of 'what you are in industry', by saying what it is that 'those people called managers do' may be replacing opacity with 'a kind of understanding'. So the book is a modest spotlight on industrial society's neglected institution.

NOTES

1 These insights and quotations are taken from a quite magnificent social and cultural history of the USA: Daniel J. Boorstin (1969). *The Americans: The National Experience*, Penguin Books, Harmondsworth.
2 This line of argument has been interestingly developed by: Michael Fores (1985) Management: Science or Activity, in Peter Lawrence and Ken Elliott (eds) *Introducing Management*, Penguin Books, Harmondsworth.
3 Daniel Boorstin, op. cit., from whose book several of these American ideas are derived.
4 In addition to the three business schools in Britain there are of course some twenty universities and more polytechnics offering first degrees in management or business administration, but these are all very recent by

American standards.

5 A more extensive discussion of the character of German management is offered in Peter Lawrence (1980) *Managers and Management in West Germany*, Croom Helm, London.

2

What Managers do all Day

In a provincial Swiss newspaper I once encountered the headline 'Alpine village scourged by Pine Martens'. At first sight this is a bit unconvincing. Although not many of us have actually seen a pine marten, pictures of them are not hard to come by. They are rather agreeable looking furry rodents, usually pictured (photographed) relaxing inoffensively in the boughs of fir trees, a pine cone their greatest delight. So where does the scourge come from?

There is a missing fact, something not generally known (even to animal photographers). It is that pine martens are irresistibly attracted by the smell of hard rubber. And having got to the rubber, they chew it! Result, vandalised car tyres and perforated radiator hoses, the collapse of private transport, community isolation, in the long term probably alpine cannibalism.

There is a similar missing fact when we try to imagine what managers do all day, at least it is missing for students. It is that all the things managers want to make happen involve other people, as means and ends. When you take this on board, the pattern of managerial activity is both clear and meaningful.

Although this simple idea of the centrality of people to management endeavour is included in most definitions of management, its practical implication for how managers actually spend their working days is usually lost. Most people, and indeed many students of management, have a picture of management as more Olympian, more impersonal, more static, and for that matter more orderly and rationally planned than it really is.

To put it another way, there is a very straight answer to the question, what do managers do all day? They go to meetings, and talk to people. Yet we have not always known this. For a long time, indeed for well over half a century after management became an established subject, no one thought to study or even make a simple record of what managers really do at work. This 'conspiracy of silence' was shattered by the work of a young Swedish economist, Sune Carlson. In the 1950s Carlson got a group of nine managing directors of companies in Sweden to keep a tightly controlled diary of their work activity for a period of a month.[1]

TRUTH STARTS IN SWEDEN

At two points Carlson's findings support the popular conception of the senior manager. First his group worked long and hard, between 8½ and 11½ hours a day; they all did work at home, and were involved in business travel. Second, what Carlson discovered confirmed the idea of the top manager as figure-head and representative of his company in the wider society, the representative function as it is known in the textbooks. This was certainly important for these managing directors, who indeed spent 44% of their working time outside or away from the company, and 33% of their working time specifically on visits and meetings at other places.

Hard work and representative duties aside the picture poduced by Carlson's research contrasted quite markedly with popular images of senior managers as studies in impersonal efficiency and lonely decision-making.

Certainly the Carlson study exploded the myth of the top manager, above the fray, absorbed in lonely contemplation of weighty policy matters. The work of these managing directors emerged as highly interactive. Taking the whole work period for a month these top managers spent an average 10% of that time working alone in their own offices, 8%

working at home, presumably work of a solitary nature – reading, thinking, drafting, and report writing, plus a further 3% of the time travelling. The rest of the time, just short of 80%, was spent working directly with others in meetings, conferences, and discussions. Moral: anyone who seeks a job 'working with people' should avoid social work (too much desk-bound administration these days) and seek to become a manager.

The other side of the coin is that these managers had, both in their view and in Carlson's, little time for reading, thinking, planning, and policy formulation. Not only did they spend a mere 10% of the total working time alone in their own offices, the obvious occasion for the discharge of these more contemplative functions, but in practice this 'own office time' was heavily fragmented. It is, that is to say, made up of lots of little periods of 5–15 minutes and therefore offered little opportunity to accomplish planning and policy tasks requiring sustained attention over time.

A related discovery is that these managers, and remember they are the top managers in their companies, were surprisingly at other people's beck and call. Their periods of work alone were typically interrupted or terminated by incoming telephone calls or the arrival of visitors, including subordinates wanting rulings or decisions. More generally the content of any day's work was determined by what the executive had in his appointments diary, but these diary entries themselves derived from the needs and demands of other people, inside and outside the company. What is more, Carlson speaks of his managers as having something of a 'diary complex', of sticking rather inflexibly to what is scheduled in the diary. Moral: if you want a senior manager to do something, make sure it goes in his diary.

Carlson also felt he identified certain inefficiencies. Where managers were members of outside bodies, part of the representative function referred to earlier, they did not really rationalise this work, so that it was more time-consuming that it need have been. Or again these managers in some cases did not organise their (frequent) absences from their own companies. It is possible to neutralise the effect of such absences by decentralising authority or to cover for them by nominating persons or committees to deputise. These responses, however, were often neglected.

A *leitmotiv* of this study is the way it revealed these very senior managers to be less formal or august in disposition than one would expect. The nature of communications is a good example. Surprisingly these top managers wrote hardly any letters, a mere two or three a week being normal. On the other hand they evinced a strong preference for verbal communication, either by telephone or face-to-face.

These managers were also curiously self-deceiving. They would often represent as temporary and unusual states of affairs which seemed to Carlson semi-permanent; they would deceive themselves about the number of hours worked (by underestimating!), and were often poor judges of the frequency or reliability with which they did things. In short, they had an impoverished understanding of their own pattern of work and its consequences.

If we keep to the content of these numerous meetings and discussions there are more surprises. To put it in general terms these meetings had much more to do with current operations, matters of application, and of problem solving, than with future developments or general policy questions. What they saw themselves as doing was continually 'getting information' in order to monitor or control events. They used this 'getting information' heading twice as frequently as any other in making the diary entries for Carlson's study.

Carlson himself felt that the neglect of policy set up a vicious circle. The executives devoted too little of their time to the formulation of policies which would guide the actions of others, resolve quandries, and circumvent problems; subordinates make frequent demands for direction and ruling or help in solving problems; the top executive has even less opportunity to develop policies which would regulate these issues, and so on.

Indeed Carlson actually coined the phrase 'administrative pathology' to signify situations where managers are conscious that what they are doing is not satisfactory but find themselves unable to change. Of course, Carlson may not necessarily be right about this; perhaps it is an instance of an academic looking at 'men of action' and seeking to order and constrain where it is not appropriate (the problem will be raised again in chapter 4). What is interesting is that this pattern of executive work is so much at odds with his orderly expectations that Carlson apostrophises it in this way. In short this pioneering study shows the work of these higher managers to be hard, highly interactive, frequently interrupted, very much oriented to the here-and-now, and to the gathering of 'hot information'!

BREVITY, VARIETY, AND FRAGMENTATION

The few studies that we have of this actual work pattern of managers tend to reinforce each other. This is certainly true of the classic American study of a group of business leaders and municipal administrators, the work of Henry Mintzberg.[2]

In a sense Mintzberg goes further than Carlson. While Carlson discovered an element of hectic disorder in the work of top managers Mintzberg frankly proclaims that management work *is* unprogrammed and that this is the essence of its challenge. It is unprogrammed in the sense that its precise content is generally unpredictable. The manager, say first thing on Monday morning, can say only that in the course of the week he will solve problems, take decisions, deal with contingencies, and talk to lots of people, but for the most part he will not be able to say what the problems and contingencies will be.

A further link between Carlson and Mintzberg is that both stress the importance of information, Mintzberg arguing that the manager's power is based on the possession of information and that this is what enables him to make sensible decisions and know what to do. At the same time Mintzberg deals another blow to the popular image of the senior manager as an aloof authority figure working in a formal way. Much of this information, that is to say, is simply a matter of finding out significant things quickly by using contacts, of piecing together a bigger picture using lots of little clues, of evaluating informal exchanges and even gossip. In other words this information is primarily in the form of oral gleanings, not written reports, memos, or computer print outs. Clearly it is Mintzberg's view that there is not much science in management, certainly in the work of top managers; it is rather a matter of oral information and semi-intuitive processes.

It goes without saying that Mintzberg sees management work as interactive, not contemplative. He also draws attention to the fact that the job of senior managers has much less formal structure than the older style textbooks suggest. Indeed it is the open-ended nature of management, the lack of structure and predictability crossed with the range of issues to be dealt with, that gives management responsibility its unrelenting nature.

Finally Mintzberg's study has revealed the pace and variety of management work. The managers in his study did not typically work in a protracted and sustained way on a small number of tasks. Instead they worked briefly on lots of different things; had a high number of contacts during the working day; picked things up, put them down, and went back to them when time permitted; endlessly shifted their attention between different people, problems, and tasks. What 'big jobs' there were tended to be handled in a fragmented way, not all in one go. Or an important issue might involve a lot of different actions, typically in the form of discussions with various groups or people, but these do not have to be carried out as an uninterrupted sequence, and they seldom are. Mintzberg encapsulated this by describing management work as characterised by brevity, variety, and fragmentation.

A BRITISH STUDY OF MANAGEMENT WORK

In contrast to these studies in Sweden and the USA the most recent research on the work of managers in Britain is a study I have made of a group of production managers and general managers in charge of manufacturing units in over 20 companies. It is a study that reinforces many of the Carlson–Mintzberg ideas, and more besides.[3]

To begin with the work of these production managers was again interactive to a high degree. Table 2.1 shows how the average distribution of time between various activities came

Table 2.1

Activity	Proportion of observed time spent on it (%)
Meetings	29.96
Ad hoc discussions	17.93
Time spent in works	17.35
Telephoning	7.23
Office work	11.16
Explanations	12.04
Total time accounted for	95.92

out. Nearly a third of the active working time was spent in formal meetings, and getting on for a fifth on *ad hoc* discussions. By the latter I mean something less formal than proper meetings, typically with fewer participants and not lasting as long. *Ad hoc* discussions are usually set up at short notice, rather than being scheduled in advance as are most formal meetings, and are more likely to deal with just one issue, rather than the series of things on the agenda of a formal meeting; they are more often oriented to some particular problem, and are sometimes used where personal hostilities between the participants might be disruptive in a more formal meeting.

The time spent telephoning is by definition interactive, and may be seen as a kind of substitute for meetings and *ad hoc* discussions; for these production managers most of the telephone calls were internal, with people in other parts of the factory or company. The category of explanations in Table 2.1 is in a sense artificial, and refers to the explanations these managers gave to me, the observer doing the study. Although this was not of course part of their normal work, it is important to put it in to show the effect of actually making the study.

The strong impression is that if I had not been there most of that 12% of working time would have been spent in more *ad hoc* discussions with colleagues and subordinates. Finally the time spent in the works, actually walking around machine shops and factory floors, was also to a large extent, interactive. A lot of this time was spent in a series of very brief exchanges with workers, foremen, inspectors, and so on, and these walks around the factory are clearly meant to facilitate communication, to give people a chance to approach the manager. The meagre 11% of working time spent by these managers on administrative or paperwork in their own offices is the other side of the picture, and the figure is strikingly consistent with that given by Carlson even though my study is of managers of a different type, in a different country and thirty years later.

VARIETY REVISITED

This British study also gives a further thrust to the idea of variety as a major feature of managerial work. To start with there is a great variety of acts and contents under each of the categories given in Table 2.1. Take formal meetings. The managers participate in these in several ways: they variously attend them, chair them, sit in as observer, go for the sake of appearances, or play a leading part in the process. The meetings are about the organisation of production, the progress of orders and deliveries to customers, or the purchase of raw materials and supplies; they are about the introduction of technical change, buying new equipment, or changing factory layouts; about liaison with the design department, the maintenance section, the production engineers, the sales force or the customers. There are meetings about quality, safety, scrap and reject sales, discipline, industrial relations, costs, expenses, profits, personnel policies, and environmental legislation. There are meetings with bosses, subordinates, other people's subordinates, and own-rank colleagues in other departments. There are special-purpose meetings, general-purpose meetings, departmental meetings, one-off meetings, and recurrent meetings.

Or consider the time spent on the shop floor by these production managers. This also serves a variety of ends, including checking work progress, the functioning of machines, the quality of the output, what is broken down and how quickly it is being repaired, and who is missing from their work post. It is an opportunity to exercise a mild disciplinary surveillance on work force and supervisors alike, note anything that is amiss, listen to reports of grievances from shop stewards and complaints from inspectors, bully anybody and everybody whose contributions are needed, and carry out a general management-by-exception role.

A RANGE OF ISSUES

This idea of variety, however, can perhaps be made more tangible with an example. Consider the activities of one of the managers in this British study, a manufacturing director in a food-processing company. In the course of 2 days this manager chaired two formal meetings, one with a dozen or so of his subordinate production managers, the other a plant-wide meeting with 25 shop stewards representing all the different trade unions on site. At both of these meetings there were six or eight items on the agenda, and the meeting with the shop stewards also involved some ticklish issues including explaining away an apparent profit windfall and heading off an undesirably large pay claim.

During the 2 days this manager had a series of smaller meetings on a range of different topics, viz.

— with one of his production managers and the maintenance manager on a major plant repair
— with the auditor sent from head office on the labelling of pallets, random checks on outgoing lorries, the control of

packaging materials, and monitoring basic raw-material usage

— with the project engineering director to discuss the programme of engineering projects and possible expenditure reductions
— with the personnel manager on how to go about replacing another manager forced to retire because of ill-health
— with another of his production managers to discuss the state of the plant, and possible personnel changes
— with another production manager to discuss output
— with the personnel manager a second time to consider a forward-looking personnel plan
— several meetings with the transport manager and the works accountant on up-dating part of the vehicle fleet, how to go about it, how much it will cost, and how to sell the idea to the European head office
— with another production manager about his budget, personnel changes, and equipment purchases
— with the purchasing manager on what to do about buying oil, the most dependable supplier having become the dearest
— with one of the production managers on how the latter's section would be run while the manager was off on a training course.

In between the meetings this manufacturing director fitted in a tour of the (extensive) plant, some report writing and cost calculations, and had 37 telephone conversations, several with the British head office in London and the European head office in Brussels.

ALL WORKING FOR THE SAME COMPANY

One effect of having a sample of managers less august than Carlson's managing directors is that the relationship between the different functions or departments – design, engineering, production, inspection, sales, finance, and so on – shows up in the pattern of management activity. These various functions are interdependent, they need each others outputs, they endlessly exchange information and coordinate joint activities. The obvious manifestation, already alluded to, is formal meetings attended by representatives of different functions for exchange or coordination purposes. So that, for example, a general manager will chair a meeting, the purpose of which is to raise product quality, and the meeting will be attended not only by people from the quality-control department (inspection), but also by designers, production managers, production engineers, and perhaps salesmen to represent the presumptive views of customers. Or the head of a design team will hold a meeting about a new product at prototype stage and the meeting will be attended by engineers who will have to figure out ways to make this product, production managers who will organise its manufacture, purchasing officers who will have to buy the necessary materials and components, and salesmen who need to know all the model's good points to urge these on eventual customers.

In fact the relations between the various functions are often far from harmonious. This stems partly from the fact that the individual departments or functions tend to take on separate identities and pursue achievement on their own terms, and sometimes expansion as well (empire building). But it is important to understand that there often are very real differences of interest between the functions, which are quite rational and not necessarily anything to do with personal ambitions or feuding for its own sake.

Take as an example the classic case of disagreements between production and sales. On just about every conceivable issue the two want different things or have different priorities:

— sales like short-lead times (= the time it takes to make something when an order for it has been placed) to impress customers; production like long-lead times to give themselves room for manoeuvre
— sales(men) like to be able to undercut stated lead times to win customers; production managers know this will make them problems

— sales like a variety of models; production like to keep it simple
— sales like to offer customers extras and modifications; production know this means hassle
— sales like frequent model changes so they can always offer the customer something new; production managers like long production runs and as few changes as possible
— salesmen are inclined to get the order first and worry about how to fill it afterwards; production people like to be sure they know how to make it before anyone tries to sell it!

The fact that there are these real differences means that managers may (be observed to) put time and effort into getting assistance and cooperation from other functions. Engineering cooperation actually becomes part of the job even though the cooperation is officially ordained. This phenomenon is quite common in the case of production managers where production often has a not entirely satisfactory relationship with design, engineering, maintenance, inspection, purchasing, and sales. In such cases it is not at all unusual to find especially junior production managers and supervisors going to all sorts of lengths to get what they want from other departments by manipulation, threats, bluff, special pleading, or horse-trading.

In extreme cases time is actually spent trying to 'frame up' other departments. In one company in which I worked the works director was so convinced that the inspection department was culpably slow in inspecting, on arrival at the company, items bought as components for the firm's manufactures, that he put his principal subordinate on to monitoring the inspection and compiling a secret dossier on the derelictions of the inspection department. The idea was that they would eventually be able to go to the managing director with 'overwhelming evidence' of inspection's failure to do its job quickly enough. In another company the sales director kept what amounted to an anthology of customer complaints about consignments of goods which were delivered late. This could always be trotted out to discredit the production department, and was a good card to play with the managing director whenever the production chief came up with some unreasonable demand, such as standardising the product range.

Finally the British study gives strong confirmation of Mintzberg's conviction that the informal and oral take priority over the formal and written. Our production managers were not for the most part great readers, writers, or drafters; the oral medium was that in which they excelled, and benign manipulation was their constant achievement.

THE ENDS SERVED

It was suggested at the beginning that the simple answer to the question, what do managers do all day, is that they go to meetings and talk to people. This answer has two merits. Firstly, it is true, and most of the empirical studies of management work give support to it. Secondly, it is an unpretentious answer, arguably more meaningful than a lot of high falutin abstraction about communication and corporate policy. The bad thing about the answer is that it is too literal, and leaves out purpose and function of the activity. In other words, what do these meetings lead to, what is all this interaction about? To some degree this question too has been answered, by naming types of meetings or giving examples of purposes achieved in discussion with others, but it may be helpful to go further.

Most of the meetings and discussions serve four ends. These four are often mixed up in practice, overlap and intermingle, but they can be separated out analytically.

INFORMATION AND COORDINATION

Information is disseminated or exchanged for the purposes of coordination. People give information to each other so that the actions of them all may be harmonised to achieve some result or have something happen in an orderly way. It is frequently a matter of harmonisation in time, in the sense that a task is broken up with parts of it being carried out by different people or groups whose contributions have to be recombined later. Or what one group is doing requires some support or phased input from others, but they have to know about it in order to provide it. Indeed they may need to know a lot of things in a lot of detail in order to make their contribution in the right form at the right time.

An example may be helpful, deliberately not quite a routine one. At a car firm where I did some work an ambitious modernisation of the paint shop (where the newly made cars are sprayed) was in train, and this gave rise to a series of meetings judged important enough to be chaired by the assistant managing director. The basic plot is that both the end-users, in this case the workers who do the painting represented by their supervisors and managers, and other people contributing to or affected by the modernisation, need to know all the facts. But there are all sorts of sub-plots.

1 The company's most modern plant is judged to be one in Belgium. A task force which has studied it reports on Belgian methods at one of these paint shop modernisation meetings.
2 There is a problem about whether with the improved paint shop three or only two coats of paint per car will be needed. This in turn has implications for the speed at which the assembly line should be run; it can be speeded up with the cars coming off more quickly if only two coats of paint are needed. And the speed of the assembly line has implications for planning the throughput in the sense of the number of finished cars per time period, and again for industrial relations, since assembly-line speed and permitted variations are written into a wage agreement.
3 Rebuilding the paint shop means rebuilding the showers, and it is suggested that the opportunity is seized to build vandal-proof showers. This, of course, has cost implications, albeit minor ones.
4 There are all sorts of practical questions including access,

vehicle handling, siting of fire doors, location of air lines and sludge lines. The general point at issue is that the people who have planned this new paint shop are different from the ones who are actually going to build it, who are different from the people who are going to use it. So that user-needs, in particular, have to be inputted to the planning and building. What is more, contingencies which at first sight are purely technical, turn out to have some human or industrial-relations meaning, which someone else will have to deal with. To give just one example, the modernisation of the paint shop will to some extent change its location, so that part of it will be next to a welding shop, which is noisy. The paint sprayers will not like this, it may become a grievance, and someone will have to take some action on it.

INFORMATION AND CONTROL

Second, information is gathered and then re-issued or applied to correct or control the actions of others. Manufacturing operations offer endless examples by compiling information on output (how many per time period), costs, quality, scrap rates, even machine utilisation and (variable) level of overtime working. Production managers then use this, often in the form of computer print outs, on their foremen to urge higher output, lower costs, less scrap, better machine utilisation, and so on. It is important to grasp that this is not just a simple exhortatory game. The foreman in question may not realise that, for example, he is spending more on overtime working, or has higher scrap rates than other foremen in their sections, unless and until someone collects the information and presents him with it. When this happens it may then be possible to pin-point causes and devise corrective measures.

A lot of meetings between sales managers and salesmen partake of this information and control operation. Most of the information collected about the salesman's performance – How many customer calls have been made over a time period? How many of these gave rise to firm orders? What was the value of these orders? – serve the ends of control. Are these salesmen in Alabama doing as well as those in Mississippi, and if not, why not; how does the sales figure for the first 3 months of 1987 compare with the same period in the year before; how is this salesman doing compared with those others; is the value of sales made up of four big orders or twenty small orders, and is the 'order-mix' changing?

SOLVING PROBLEMS

The *raison d'être* for many meetings and exchanges is the actual or presumptive existence of problems. So that the thrust of the meeting may be to find out if there is a problem, where it is, and what to do about it. Again manufacturing operations offer recurrent examples of this phenomenon, a standard one being what are called production-control meetings. Participants at these meetings review the progress of various jobs and check them against the dates on which the finished job has been promised to a customer, this operation being predicated on the assumption that some of the jobs will be running late. So it becomes a question of establishing which jobs, how late, and what to do about them (there are endless remedies in this situation, but you need to know how and when to apply them).

Or to take something less routine, at a brewery in West Germany where I did a research project the accountants computed a 6% shortfall in sales compared with the previous year. This fact was presented to the production managers as a challenge requiring a corresponding cost-cutting response. At the ensuing production–finance meeting various money-saving expedients were generated – non-replacement of retiring workers, reduction of overtime working, reduced energy costs, and so on – and at the same time the participants generated some positive ideas which might push sales back up again.

Or again, at a food-processing company in West Germany I witnessed the 'final solution' to a middle-term quality problem centring on degeneration of the critical raw material at a particular point in the process. In this case the problem was confronted by all the interested parties plus a head-office specialist. The meeting threw up a hypothesis to explain the degeneration, set up and executed instant chemical tests, which actually disconfirmed the hypothesis, developed a new hypothesis which was confirmed by tests, and then having established a cause collectively developed a remedy.

DEVISING FUTURE INITIATIVES

A lot of the management literature is devoted to the function of planning. This is misleading in my view because planning is something that most companies do not do most of the time (perhaps they should, but . . .). Devising future initiatives is in fact much more intermittent and selective. What tends to happen is that so long as things are going well, one does not plan; one simply hopes that the future will be a continuation of the (highly satisfactory) present. But when a problem, threat, or challenge emerges, this gives rise to at least an episode of targeted planning.

Consider the case of a German engineering company which made one of its products in a light metal alloy. All went well until a rival company began to manufacture the same item in the same alloy, and made a superior job of it. The first company held a meeting attended by research scientists, production managers, and sales people to decide what their future response would be. They decided not to adopt any of the business-tactic options – splitting the market with the rival company, buying it out, making its product under licence, ceasing to compete in this particular product line, and so on – and concentrated instead on how to produce an even better product in the light alloy material, one which would restore their market lead. This resolution in turn led to questions of time, cost, materials, specialisation, and (design) points of comparative advantage.

One feature of this kind of endeavour, that of constructing future initiatives, is that it frequently calls for the pooling of perspective and expertise by people from different functions.

So far the tendency has been to depict management work in a rather monolithic way, as though all managers are subject to the same constraints, are animated by the same dynamics. This is only partly true, and the aim of the next chapter must be to redress the balance somewhat by looking in more detail at managers specialising in different areas of management work.

NOTES

1 For this pioneering study of the actual work of top managers see Sune Carlson (1951) *Executive Behaviour*, Strömberg, Stockholm. It should be said that this book is rather difficult to get hold of, but in Britain at least a copy is held by the British Lending Library at Boston Spa.

2 Henry Mintzberg (1973) *The Nature of Managerial Work*, Harper & Row, New York.

3 This study of the work of general and production managers is presented in more detail in Peter Lawrence (1984) *Management in Action*, Routledge & Kegan Paul, London. A further interest of this book is that it compares groups of managers in Britain and West Germany.

3

The Chequer Board

"Fancy this Englishman coming a thousand miles to study your Fascist methods, Dad", observed the son of a German manager in whose company I spent a few days (the father quoted this remark with evident satisfaction). This manager did indeed lay on a good performance including a draconian inspection of the works, confrontation with other management colleagues, savage cost-cutting measures, and illicit (counter to group policy) second-hand equipment deals on the side. The morning, which began with his telling the marketing director, much his senior: 'Now I've seen how you go about things I understand why this company is threatened with short time working', ended on the factory roof investigating a presumed structural fault while Boeing 737s passed some 50 feet above as they angled in to Munich airport. In the evening we relaxed at a re-union meeting of his student duelling society!

The point is not to offer a pen portrait of German management: this firebrand behaviour is as untypical there as it is in Britain or the USA, except perhaps for the willingness to confront seniors with criticism.[1] It shows, rather, something more fundamental. That most situations in life offer a choice, and most jobs in management certainly do. One can behave in this way or that way, put the emphasis here rather than there, make X the priority rather than Y or Z, make a splash with one part of the job rather than another, and so on.

The main thrust of the previous chapter was to argue that the reality of management work is rather different from its popular image, that it is more hectic, short term, problem oriented, interactive, and fragmented than most people think. On the other hand this line of argument does tend to obscure the element of choice, the fact that different kinds of management work, and the possibility of different patterns of activity as between these jobs. The aim of this chapter is to redress the balance, by outlining the range of management jobs and specialisms, and by giving some idea of how they fit together.

THE HOUSE THAT JACK BUILT

There is not really any such thing as 'a typical company' so an idealised organisation chart will not really help.[2] Company structure is a lot of ifs and buts, and it is easier to sort them out in prose than in diagrams.

The place to start is the middle, with production, rather than the beginning, because there are alternative beginnings. The generic name for companies which make and sell goods is manufacturing companies. By definition they all have a production facility, a part or parts of the company where goods are made, though they may not make the whole product, or all of their products.

Sometimes companies sub-contract parts of the manufacturing operation; that is, they pay other usually smaller companies to do it for them. Occasionally companies have (some of) their finished products made by other firms with the firm placing the order having its brand name on the produce.

The production part of the firm is where the bulk of the labour force is employed, their work being overseen by what are called foremen in traditional firms and first-line supervisors in 'new look' companies. The rank above the foreman is often, but not always, known as that of production superintendent. Above the superintendent rank, depending on the size and organisation of the company, there may be other levels in the production management hierarchy culminating in a works director, manufacturing director, or production director. If the particular factory one is looking at is not the whole company, but one of many separate works or plants making up the company, then the top managers there will not be directors, or at least not directors in the legal sense even if they have the courtesy title. The manager with the highest responsibility for production in such one-among-several works is more likely to have a title such as works manager or plant manager.

It is impossible to talk about the way companies are put together without using these ranks and titles as a matter of convenience. At the same time it is important to emphasise that these titles are not standardised. Job titles in management are not fixed like ranks in the army, and they vary a lot in practice. To give an example, the title plant manager in Imperial Chemicals Industry (ICI) denotes the first rank in the production hierarchy above the level of foreman; in the Ford Motor Company the plant manager is the overall head of a complete manufacturing entity, equal to a managing director of a big firm elsewhere.

A STAR IS BORN

So much for production, but what precedes it? There are several answers to this. The textbook answer is that there will be some process or activities whereby products are researched, discovered, invented, developed, or designed. What it comes down to is that in the science-based industries such as chemicals, petroleum, pharmaceuticals, electronics, and telecommunications, there is Research and Development (R&D), where the research shows a product or process to be scientifically possible and the development gets it from an idea to something tangible and operationally viable. In the engineering industry – cars, planes, ships, machine tools, instruments, and equipment and machinery of many kinds – production is preceded by design. Design is a composite and variable activity. It embraces a creative process in the sense of imagining or conceiving of new products or models, thinking what they would look like and what features they would have and then drawing them, and doing all the calculations and going on to make (machine) drawings of them.

Does this mean that all companies have an R&D or design function? No, it does not. There are some products which are so simple and/or unchanging that no design is required. These products may have been designed by someone 'once upon a time', but design is not a continuous process. Another common occurrence is that the R&D function is physically separated from the rest of the works, so that it exists, but not only the workers but most of the managers never actually see it. There is something like a tradition in Britain whereby R&D establishments are located in country houses in their own grounds, and preferably in areas that graduates like to live in – the south and the Thames Valley. In the USA there are similar clusterings of research in the choicer bits of New England and in Southern California.

This segregation of research or design may also assume international dimensions. Much of the machine-tool (lathes, milling and drilling machines, borers, etc.) industry in Britain is American owned so that many of these British works are making and selling products designed in the USA. Or to give a more generalised example, companies have all sorts of reasons for establishing manufacturing operations in the Third World but they seldom situate the R&D there; this remains firmly in North America or Western Europe.

BETWEEN CONCEIVING AND MAKING

In much of industry, especially that producing three-dimensional artefacts, there is another phase between design and production. This is the figuring out how to make it, or make it quickly, cheaply, and in large numbers. Design usually stops with the production of a model or a prototype; it is then up to engineers to devise methods for commencing production. The function is usually referred to as production engineering, or sometimes process engineering.

In industries where periodic product or model changes are normal, the automobile industry is an excellent example, the whole operation is phased, in a planned sequence. First there is the design phase, then the production engineering phase, then actual production in large numbers. And all the while the marketing department is striving to create demand and take orders.

END OF THE TRAIL?

Selling the goods, which at least logically is the end of the story, is a strangely variable activity. In the popular mind it is the work of wonderfully persuasive individuals working on other people who end up buying things. This idea is not wrong but rather incomplete. Direct selling by very persuasive salesmen certainly occurs; it is the 'missionary selling' of American textbooks, especially where the customers are buying whatever it is for the first time. But there are two important departures from this attractively straightforward model.

First, the relative importance of direct selling, what salesmen do, varies a lot from industry to industry. In some cases promotional advertising may be made more important than anything salesmen do; or selling may be more the result of the way the distribution system is organised, perhaps a simple matter of easy availability matching established demand. Little cardboard trays of potato chips, for instance, are available from kiosks in every town square in Belgium without anyone actually selling them in the sense that encylopaedias are sold. Probably the important generalisation on this matter is that personal selling tends to be more important for industrial goods and less important for consumer goods.

Second, a lot of selling is more routine than outsiders think; it is the re-order selling of the marketing textbooks. In a lot of cases, that is, the big question is not: will this person buy? It is rather, when will they place the order, for how much, or what mix of goods will they want? Consider for instance that companies that make electrical consumer goods must buy paint, they cannot dispatch fridge-freezers gift wrapped in crepe paper. And unless there is a good reason why not, such a company will buy the paint from the same source as previously, and the questions really are when, how much, and perhaps what kind?

Sales, like R&D, tend to get physically segregated from the manufacturing part of the company. Salesmen naturally spend much time 'on the road', and use their homes and cars as offices, rather than the office space allocated to them at the company. Or again sales echelons are often organised in a separate way, the sales function being located at head office, or at a separate sales administration centre. Or again many companies which manufacture only in their home country sell abroad and have sales and service formations in these foreign countries which are by definition divorced from the works.

The idea that many people have of the salesman, dynamic and proactive, misses something else. This is that especially in industries where the emphasis is on personal selling the salesman puts a lot of ingenuity into getting information. There is no end to the things the salesman wants to know.

There is a need to identify potential customers. Who uses, who needs, and better still who *really* needs (but does not know it yet) the goods or services being sold. And if these potential customers are organisations – companies, government departments, public utilities, or whatever – rather than simply individual members of the general public, then there is a need to know relevant things about these organisations. Who are the various people the salesmen meets on his forays into them, how much have they got to spend, what do they really need, what will turn on whom, when is the end of their financial year (and how pressing is their need to buy)? Perhaps some of these ideas can be brought into focus by saying that a salesman, visiting a company to which he hopes to sell, is looking all the time for the MAN. The MAN is that person in the organisation who has the Money, the Authority to spend it, and the Need for the product or service.

It was suggested at the beginning that sales came after manufacturing, at least logically. It does, but the temporal order may not be the same as the logical. There are many cases, that is, where the selling comes before the making, sometimes before even the designing. Clearly this is often true in the generalised sense that a company will do market research to establish the existence of a demand for something, perhaps something which the company does not know how to make and has not even invented at that stage. So, for instance, pharmaceutical companies do not embark on long and costly research programmes to develop, say, a drug to combat asthma without being convinced that there are people whom it will benefit (there is a demand!). But this is also often true in a quite particularist way. Bespoke tailors, for example, do not make and sell suits (in that order). They sell the idea that they can make the suit a customer wants, take the order, and then make it. Or again Boeing does not make 757s on spec, but for known customers who have placed orders.

So far the various functions of a manufacturing company have been identified in a logical sequence; R&D or design, process or production engineering, manufacturing, sales. This logical sequence, however, is not the whole story. It omits two categories of function, those which are outside the sequence, in a sideways–on relation to it, and also an assemblage of specialist activities surrounding the production operation.

PRODUCTION'S SUPPORTING CAST

Variety and heterogeneity are themes of this book: different management functions, different styles, the absence of standardised job titles, and differences in organisational structure. The last of these, differences in structure, can be illustrated very well by the way production is organised. So far we have noted the design – production engineering – manufacturing sequence, but there are other specialised activities that support production.

Although the manufacturing companies which buy raw materials in the strict sense of the term – iron, steel, other metals, coal, oil, rubber, and so on – are probably a minority, almost all companies buy something as inputs to their own manufacturing process, usually in the form of parts, components, extras, and sub-assemblies. In all but the smallest companies these buying activities are handled by a specialist purchasing section.

This brings us to the first piece of organisational variety.

Most of these purchasing sections are independent in an organisational sense, in that they report to their own purchasing director, or the senior purchasing manager reports directly to the managing director, as in figure 3.1. But a substantial minority of purchasing departments are under the control of the production function; that is, the person responsible for purchasing reports to a senior production manager (see figure 3.2 below). Either arrangement can be defended. Production-controlled purchasing makes for an emphasis on punctuality and reliability in the sense of all the parts needed for production arriving in the right numbers at the right time. Independent purchasing, on the other hand, favours a better performance of the more discretionary parts of the buying job – better market information, knowing about alternative suppliers, advance knowledge of gluts, scarcities, and price trends, and so on. There is a mild trend in Britain towards independent purchasing departments which was revealed a few years ago in a survey by the British Institute of Management.[3] At the same time senior production managers who do not control the purchasing function are often critical of it, and keen to get their hands on it.[4]

People tend to think of inspection as coming at the end of the sequence, of finished goods being checked over before being sent to the customers, and this is quite right. But the quality-control or quality-assurance department, as inspection is usually called, plays a part at the beginning of the sequence as well. More often than not, that is, purchased parts or materials are inspected on arrival at the company which has bought them before they are released for use in production. In some companies, depending on the nature of the product, the quality-control department may make medial checks as well; may inspect or test things at intermediate stages of manufacture. In the process industries – chemicals, pharmaceuticals, oil refining, brewing, food processing – the inspection is typically in the form of laboratory tests or analyses. In the engineering industries it is more in the form of, putting it simply, measuring bits of metal and testing the moving parts. In either case, the quality-control function is usually independent in the sense discussed already

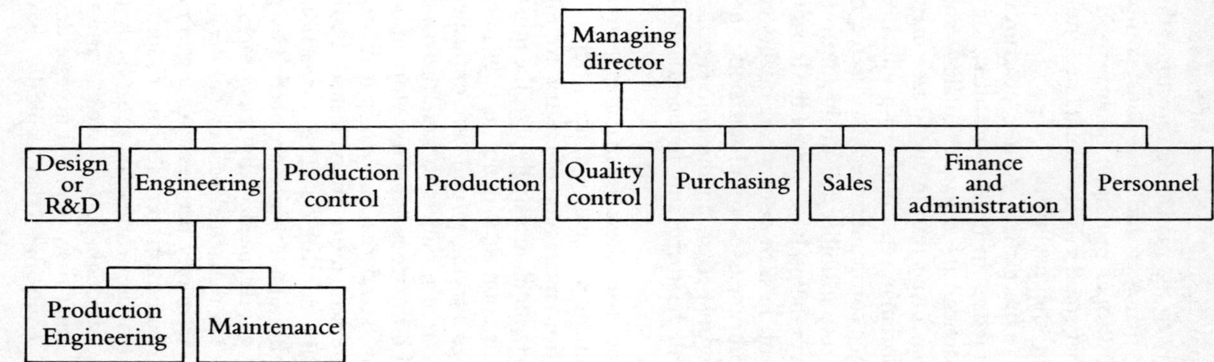

Figure 3.1 Production: The slim-line model

with regard to purchasing, that is, it reports to its own director or directly to the managing director rather than to a senior production manager. Indeed in most companies this is a point of constitutional principle: quality control must be independent so that standards are maintained, no one should be able to 'lean on' the inspectors.

As one might expect there some departures from this pristine line in practice. In little companies, for instance, it may not be practical to separate quality control from production, so that inspection in such cases may be a small section run by a foreman reporting to a production manager. And in some larger companies there has been a move in the 1980s to putting responsibility for quality into the hands of production workers themselves, part of the learning from the Japanese movement. In such cases where quality control as an activity/responsibility passes to production, there are still likely to be a few inspectors in the conventional sense but although they will be there and independent their role is attenuated.

More important than these formal departures from the model of an independent quality-control department is the fact that production managers often try to influence the quality-control personnel informally. For the most part this is not as sinister as it sounds; it is not usually in the form of production managers trying to pull rank on inspectors to get them to pass defective products to save the hassle of doing them again (though this does happen). More often it is about speed rather than standards. Or to put it another way production managers are more often incensed by the slowness with which quality control do their inspections, both of components bought outside which are needed by production, and of finished goods needed by customers. It is this slowness, rather than the actual pass or fail decisions, which give rise to most acrimony between production and quality control. So production managers seeking to influence events in the quality-control department are most likely to be trying to speed up the through-put of work, and prioritising particular jobs (do that first, we need it yesterday).

Manufacturing companies also typically have what is

known as a production-control section. In a situation, very common, where the company is making different things for different customers in different numbers (15 of X for customer A, 27 of Y for customer B, and so on), all of it to different deadlines, the function of production control is to decide what jobs will be done in what numbers in what order to which deadlines, and then try to make it happen.

A variation on the theme is that in process industries production control is more usually called production planning. A working definition of process industry is that its output is dimensional rather than integral. The output, that is, has to be measured; it is, for example, *x* tons of nitrate fertiliser, *y* gallons of refined oil, *z* cubic feet of carbon dioxide gas. Whereas the output of non-process industries can be counted as discrete units; it is 17 forklift trucks, a Boeing 747 every 9 days, a BMW car every 40 seconds, or whatever. In process industries the capacity of the plant can be varied to suit the output required, so that the relevant operation is literally one of production planning (setting the plant to meet the required output) rather than production control.

Whether we speak of production planning or production control, this is yet another function which is sometimes organisationally independent (figure 3.1), and sometimes under the control of a more senior production manager (figure 3.2). The latter arrangement is probably most common, and in any case this relationship between production and production control is not usually especially tense or acrimonious, unlike that between production and maintenance.

The importance of the maintenance section, charged with maintaining and repairing plant, equipment, and machines, varies considerably in practice. It is most important in process industries which practice near continuous production (run all the time) and in assembly-line mass production where breakdowns affecting the line may stop everything. With regard to the way maintenance as a function is fitted into the organisation it is the reverse of production control; sometimes, that is, it is under the control of a production manager as in figure 3.2, but more often than not it is formally

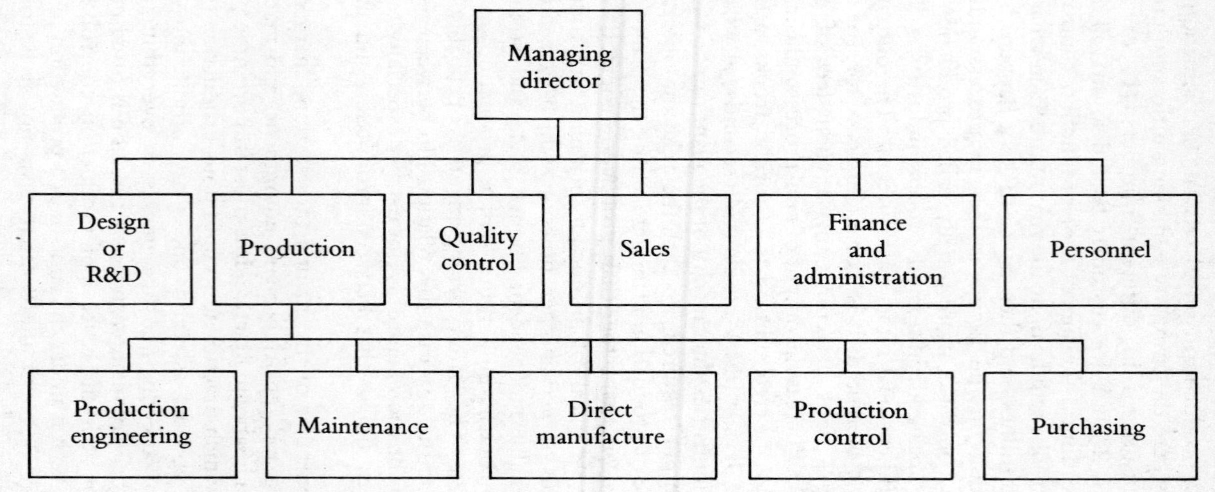

Figure 3.2 Production conquers all

independent of the production function reporting to a separate engineering director (figure 3.1).

Again there is recent survey evidence in Britain to suggest that when maintenance is not controlled by production criticism of the maintenance service is common, and senior production managers are keen to get control of maintenance.[5] Maintenance bosses on their side are quite ready to counter-attack with indictments of machine abuse, technical ignorance, and the naive proclivity of production managers to want to see 3-week plant overhauls conducted in 20 minutes.

This often tense situation is sometimes made worse by the fact that the maintenance function is under-resourced. There is something of a reluctance in Britain to spend money on maintenance, which is by definition non-productive. Again in Britain in many companies there is a social status cleavage between production workers and maintenance workers, the former being only semi-skilled while the latter are often skilled ex-apprentices. What is more the cleavage may be reinforced by dependence, where the production workers depend on maintenance fitters for machine settings, adjustments, and repairs. There is a very entertaining account by a French sociologist of just such a situation in a French cigarette factory, where the maintenance fitters and production workers are at daggers drawn. The maintenance fitters go swashbuckling their way around the works, and enhance this effect of their special skills by always refusing to give explanations and actually confiscating the repair manuals![6]

Before taking up the theme of chapter 2, the nature of management work, this time with an awareness of the range of different management jobs in industry, it will be helpful to consider three more specialist functions, personnel, and finance, and management services.

SYSTEMATISING PEOPLE

It is possible to argue about whether or not personnel is a specialist function. Its mission, broadly defined, is one of looking after people, but others outside the personnel function can do this, and on occasion do. After all, sales managers look after their salesmen, accountants in the finance and administration department control their subordinates, assistants, and secretaries, and production managers are responsible for vast numbers of blue-collar workers. So what is different about personnel, and why do we have personnel departments?

Personnel needs to be understood in a wider context. It is something of a buffer between the company and society in the sense that the existence of a personnel department is some guarantee of decent standards and practices. It is implicitly telling the world that the company is both civilised and rational in its treatment of people. It is the personnel function which absorbs any anti-capitalist or anti-industrialist sentiment in the wider society.

Personnel is also a link between the company and society, at several levels. At the most general level personnel is society's window into the firm, informing companies of standards, expectations, and aspirations of its employees as they come from the wider world. At a more tangible level, of course, personnel is the link with the outside society as a labour market; personnel hires employees, and needs to know not only the techniques but the going rates. In particular personnel departments are a link between companies and society's education system. Personnel knows how that system works, what its grades and qualifications mean, how to recruit trained electricians, engineers, business graduates, and trainee draughtsmen. Personnel also knows how to plug into the national educational system and where to send who for what training. And of course personnel knows the law, or that part of it relating to business enterprises, and changes in that law. So that the personnel department is expected to know, for instance, about safety legislation, employee rights, changes in the law affecting industrial relations, and to be able to advise line managers on these things.

But above all the strength of personnel departments is that they 'do it systematically'. Personnel managers have become experts in servicing people. Other managers, especially production managers, do some of these people-servicing things, but they do it in an *ad hoc* way, with an eye to immediate convenience and often with a short-time perspective. It is by doing it in a systematic way that personnel scores. They administer pay and pension schemes, and run welfare facilities. They keep records, systematise recruitment, standardise application forms, keep tabs on employees and know for what they are eligible and when. They know the law, know the procedures, and know the labour market, and they understand these things better than hard-pressed production managers who are trying to get the work done and do personnel administration on the side.

It is interesting that personnel is a high-profile function. Just to take one indicator, personnel is an area of management work that people at school have heard of and often express an interest in. It is visible, because of its societal-links function, but it also enjoys esteem with the educational outsider because of a high degee of professionalisation. Personnel work abounds in techniques and procedures – selection and recruitment techniques, job descriptions, training manuals, employee-performance appraisal schemes, job analysis, career-development programmes, and so on – and these are seen not only as tools for doing the job but as the accoutrements of professional status *per se*.

CARRY ON COUNTING

In the management textbooks it will tell you that the finance or finance and administration department is responsible for a company's capitalisation. This is true, yet share issues and other acts of capital restructuring are not exactly everyday events, and the work of finance departments tends to consist of activities both more recurrent and more homely.

First, finance departments pay people. Most obviously they organise the payment of wages and salaries to employees. Actually calculating the wages of employees may be complicated by a piece-work system, or by a plethora of extras and deductions. Then finance has to discharge the company's outside debts, not only to government and taxation authorities but to a host of suppliers. Finance will also be concerned with the terms of deals with suppliers: is there a discount, is payment phased over time, is there a reduction for prompt settlement and if not for how long can settlement be deferred?

Finance also has the corresponding duty to collect money owing to the company, in other words to send invoices to customers and get the money out of them. This in turn implies what is called a credit-control function, deciding whether potential customers are financially sound enough to be supplied on credit.

Second, finance has the awesome duty of analysing profitability. Outsiders would be amazed to know how much effort and ingenuity goes into this activity. Knowing that the company has made, say, a pre-tax profit of £70 million is not the end of the story but the beginning. It raises questions, such as how does this year's figure compare with last year's, why is it different, and will close study reveal underlying trends? But above all is the need to know where the profit comes from. What divisions, works, or parts of the company contribute most. What products or which product ranges are most profitable. How does profit originate geographically, are manufacturing operations in the Third World more profitable than those in the USA, are sales in Western Europe yielding higher profit levels than those in Australia, and so on.

Third, finance is responsible for cash-flow management at company level, for seeing that the company has enough ready money for current outgoings, especially wages and payments to suppliers. This is ususally achieved by an amalgam of paying all bills as late as possible, spacing out payments, pressuring the company's own debtors to pay up quickly, and judicious borrowing, especially short-term borrowing. With regard to the last it should be added that a large company will not simply have 'a bank' but will deal with many banks; there will be competition among banks to lend to a substantial company, and interest rates will be favourable.

Those who work in finance are mostly accountants, trainee accountants, or 'office juniors' under the direction of accountants. In this sense it is another very professionalised area of management work. Finance is also a well-known route to the top. Or to put it more precisely, a disproportionate number of managing directors have a finance background.

The world recession of the 1980s, by making money scarce and business more competitive, has raised the status of finance. It has also caused a shift in emphasis in the direction of avoiding over commitment or vulnerability at all costs.

IN WHICH WE SERVE

The last 20 years have seen the growth of management-services departments in larger companies, these being based around the advancing capabilities of computers and software.

The primary function of these management-services departments is devising what are known as management-information systems. A management-information system is a computer-based arrangement for processing and then representing information in a systematic way, the output being of assistance to managers in exercising control or taking decisions. So, for instance, many aspects of the production operation may be the object of these information systems – cost breakdowns, values of stocks of raw materials held, distribution of available costs between different products, and so on. The same applies to sales/market information where the input to the information system may be raw data about who has sold what to whom when at what price, and the output is processed information showing most profitable product lines, sales areas, particular customers, or even types of deal.

Overlapping with the management-information systems function is the role of management-services departments in helping to solve any problems that are susceptible to computer-aided quantitative methods. The management-services department, for instance, may devise or improve production-control systems (see earlier discussion of production control under the heading of 'Production's supporting cast'). Or perhaps there is a problem about how much stock of components to hold, in balancing the costs of holding the stock against the risk of running out of some item and having to stop production. Given such a challenge management-services people might investigate usage rates and holding costs and come up with a computer program which tells users when to re-order which items in what quantities.

In earlier years management-services departments were staffed by a mixture of non-graduates trained in computer programming or systems analysis, and mostly science and maths graduates with some postgraduate computer training. Nowadays it is more a question of computer science graduates, or maths or management science graduates whose undergraduate course included some computer specialisation.

The account given here is perhaps too monochrome in the sense of relating the operations of the management-services departments to the computer and associated software. Some companies have a more multi-competent management-services department in which different kinds of specialists are based, so that there may be economists and statisticians working on business forecasts, specialists in corporate strategy, organisational design, or in management development, as well as computer-systems people.

So far a considerable range of management jobs has been indicated, in the areas of R&D, design, production engineering, production, purchasing, production control or production planning, maintenance, quality control, sales, personnel finance, and finally management services. At the same time some progress has been made in showing how these functions fit together, particularly how the output of one is an input for the other. So that, for example, purchasing and maintenance serve production, quality control serves sales by guaranteeing standards, and personnel serves everyone.

In the last part of this chapter the aim is to take up the 'what managers do all day' theme of the previous chapter and examine it in the new light of our chequer-board picture of management specialisms.

PLUS ÇA CHANGE?

In the previous chapter management activity was depicted in a particular way, and this was done with reference to some pieces of research on top managers in Sweden and the USA and on general and production managers in Britain. That perhaps rather monolithic picture of management has now been relativised somewhat.

At the head of companies are a small number of top managers, managing directors in English, chief executive officers in American. Below them are general managers: this term is not precise but is usually used to designate managers in charge of complete units, typically manufacturing units, to refer to fairly senior managers responsible for a *variety* of functions, not just, say, sales, or R&D, on its own. Below these general managers come managers from the range of functions outlined in this chapter, and below them a miscellany of workers, fitters, clerks, assistants, technicians, and secretaries.

It was suggested earlier that the work of managers is hectic, short term, problem oriented, interactive, and fragmented. Now that we have indicated the range of management jobs across a variety of functions the question arises, is the pattern of work the same for all of them?

There is one straightforward and common-sense way in which it clearly is not. Managers in these different functions are actually working on different things. The content of their work is different: one is seeing suppliers and arranging the terms of purchase deals, another is coordinating the work of a group of designers, while yet another is organising the work of salesmen in a particular territorial area, and so on.

What is more it is only fair to say that there are differences in the pattern and attributes of the work that go beyond straightforward differences of content or immediate objective. The person who has sought to illuminate these differences among types of management work is the British management writer and researcher, Rosemary Stewart, and she has done so in a series of studies.

The first of these studies by Rosemary Stewart is of the work of some 160 managers in Britain.[7] This sample of 160 is a complete cross section: managers from different companies and different hierarchic levels, and distributed over several functions and specialisms, with a corresponding variety of job titles – including general manager, chief executive, chief engineer, accountant, sales manager, marketing director.

The most general finding to come out of this study is that there are all sorts of differences in the way these managers spend their time. The actual number of hours worked per week differs markedly across the sample, ranging from 35 to 60. There was a similar difference in the places where they worked – head office, own factory or works, own office, other managers' offices, or even outside the company altogether. In particular the proportion of time spent on paperwork varied considerably, with the mean figure for the sample being 36% but with some of the sample spending less than 20% and some over 60% on this activity.

Rosemary Stewart revealed similar differences with regard to the interactive elements of the manager's work. The mean figure for time spent working alone was 33% for her sample, compared with only 10% for the Carlson and Lawrence samples, but with four managers spending less than 10% of their time working alone at one extreme, and another four spending more than 70% of their time working alone at the other extreme. Similarly the amount of time a manager spent with his boss also varied: the mean figure is 8%, yet eight managers in the sample spent over a fifth of their whole working time in this way while another 15 spent no time at all with their boss.

Furthermore, Rosemary Stewart's findings also threw some doubt on Mintzberg's idea that management work is characterised by variety and fragmentation. She very cleverly shows that the *degree* of variety itself varies, this point being made by contrasting in percentage terms the difference between managers' minimum and maximum weeks. To give just one example, with regard to time spent in their own office, 51 of the managers, nearly a third of the sample, showed differences of 10–30% between the minimum and maximum weeks. On the subject of fragmentation Rosemary Stewart was able to show considerable differences in the number and frequency of interruptions, or to put it another way, differences in the number of uninterrupted half-hour periods in a working month. In other words, Rosemary Stewart has treated variety and fragmentation as variables rather fundamentals of management work.

RECONCILING THE UNRECONCILABLE

The difference between the picture of management work produced by earlier researches and that of Rosemary Stewart is striking: can they be reconciled? There is, I think, a quite viable explanation. This is that there is a clear line running from top management through general management and several levels in the production-management hierarchy and indeed down to the supervisor level, and that jobs on this line have the classic features of brevity, variety, and fragmentation, and are indeed highly interactive, problem-oriented, and hot-information dependent. Away from that line there is a lot of variation, and it matters a good deal whether one is talking about an R&D manager or a production controller, an accountant or a chief engineer, a market research manager or a maintenance boss.

This interpretation actually finds some support from a later study of management work by Rosemary Stewart, again with a (functionally and hierarchically) mixed sample of managers.[8] This is a sophisticated and quite complicated study, but to simplify it somewhat, Rosemary Stewart classifies the work of managers in two ways. The first classification is according to the manager's contacts, their direction, scope, and frequency. This covers questions such as: with whom does the manager have contacts, are they with his superiors, his subordinates, his equals, his equals in other functions, or even other people's superiors and subordinates; is the direction of contract upwards, downwards, or sideways; are these contacts with people inside or outside the organisations?

Rosemary Stewart's second classification in this later study is in terms of work-pattern characteristics, in brief: the duration of activities, the time span of decisions, the extent to which tasks are periodic or recurrent, the ratio between expected and unexpected work elements, the incidence of urgent work or crises, the prevalence of deadlines, and the origin of activities in the sense that they might arise in response to the needs of others or be self-generated. These two sets of classifications, contacts and characteristiscs, are then combined to yield four general management work patterns. These four patterns do not coincide exactly with work in the various functions outlined earlier in the chapter, still less with job-title labels, but there is some overlap.

Pattern One is Systems Maintenance

The work pattern for these systems-maintenance jobs is generally recurrent, fragmented, responding, trouble-shooting, and Rosemary Stewart illustrates it with production manager and branch manager jobs in her sample. This kind of work involves monitoring to see that targets are being met, dealing with disturbances to the system which might threaten the attainment of objectives, handling exceptions, and responding to problems as they arise. This is good traditional Carlson–Mintzberg–Lawrence stuff.

Pattern Two is System Administration

This is a sharp contrast to Pattern One. The work is recurrent, externally imposed deadlines are important, the work may contain a predominance of either expected or unexpected elements but because it is a system which is being administered it is more stable and orderly than the previous type and with less trouble-shooting. Accountants and financial managers are the examples *par excellence* from the sample.

Pattern Three is Project Work

Project work is non-recurrent, long term, and requires

sustained attention. It is characterised by long-term tasks of a one-off nature, and relatively little time will be spent responding to system demands or to other people's wants. The perfect example is the job of R&D manager, but Rosemary Stewart also gives as examples from her sample the jobs of product sales manager, group product manager, and project leader.

Pattern Four is Mixed Work

Quite simply it has no dominant characteristics. The examples Rosemary Stewart gives from the sample are such posts as general manager, area sales manager, head of administration, and product engineer. Jobs of this kind are more likely to be in senior management, and to offer considerable choice as to work pattern.

HORSES FOR COURSES

Very engaging in connection with the four work patterns are Rosemay Stewart's observations on their implications for people. Systems Maintenance suits those who are energetic, resourceful, and decisive (and possibly restless!). Systems Administration suits those who like security and can adapt to deadlines. The Project work pattern suits those who can maintain interest and momentum over long periods and be self-generating. And then the sombre warning: Work Pattern One and Work Pattern Two are habit forming. You could become a security freak or a crisis junkie.

EMBARRAS DE CHOIX

Lastly we would like to return to the idea introduced at the start of the chapter, that of choice in management jobs. The exercise of this choice may also lead to variability in management work. Again the best treatment of this subject is undoubtedly that provided by Rosemary Stewart in her most recent book.[9] In a sentence, her thesis is that all management jobs contain some demands, and are surrounded by certain constraints, but in between the two is a variable degree of choice. It is this choice which is our present concern.

Demands are present in all management jobs in the sense that a minimum job performance has to be achieved. The salesman has to sell something, the maintenance manager has to get some of the repairs done, the research manager has to produce some ideas. What is more in most management jobs there are some elements which cannot be avoided in any way, they cannot be delegated or ignored. There are meetings which one has to go to, procedures which cannot be side-stepped, reports that have to be written, data which have to be collected, calculations and costings which have to be made, and so on. On the other side there are constraints, some limitations on what can be done, how and when. To take the obvious example, resources are limited – time, money, space, people, and equipment. But there may also be constraints imposed by the environment, the law, maybe by trade-union practice or even by people's expectations. Between the demands and the constraints, however, there will be choice, in varying degree but always present. This choice may be exercised in terms of what to do and how to do it. Let us start with what.

INTERPRETATION AT WORK

Management jobs are complex, by definition they contain various elements, so that one may choose to give relative emphasis to this rather than to that. Most management jobs involve both technical and supervisory elements; one may choose to give priority to the one or the other. Most managers have subordinates, but they can choose how much time to spend with them; what is more there is a further choice about the relationship with subordinates in the sense that one can choose to control them enough to get the work done or one may take on a responsibility for their development as junior managers. No management job is completely risk-free yet risk-averse managers can do much to avoid taking risks: they keep their heads down, stick to procedures, play it by the book, or refer it to someone else to decide. On the other hand risk-lovers can go ahead and take risks, and there is an 'initiative-is-a-good-thing' ideology conveniently at hand to justify it.

It is the same with change and innovation. All management jobs offer some scope for engineering change or engaging in innovation, even jobs of the more routine and procedural systems administration kind. One may always consider changing the system, or if that is too revolutionary, refining the system or streamlining it. Or one may have constructive dialogue with those who use the output of the system and improve 'consumer satisfaction'. On the other hand relatively few management jobs actually impel change. It is a choice. So is what Rosemary Stewart calls boundary maintenance.

A manager may think it important to protect the unit he is in charge of against undue disturbance or disruption from without. This protective function is boundary maintenance. It involves warding off unreasonable demands from bosses or other departments, preventing resource cuts, neutralising rubbish-orders that come down the line from head office, or wherever. Yet not all managers do this. Some are too scared, or too naive, or think it is wrong, or are too busy doing some other part of the job they think is more important.

What is more delegation is choice. Textbooks tend to work on a Hamlet model where delegation is concerned. To delegate or not to delegate, that is the question. Usually, however, it is not the most important question. The most important question for a manager is what to delegate. Should he delegate the trouble-shooting because it scares him, or the routine because it bores him? Should he hold on to the discretionary element because that is what he is paid for, or delegate it and let someone else take the blame for the foul-ups? Should he hold on to the innovation part of the job, or pass it on to some bright young PhD and use his middle-aged guile to get the systems maintenance bit right?

MEANS TO ENDS

There is also a choice element in how management jobs are done. One can, for instance, vary the degree of formality in contacts and relationships. One can live with a high degree of fragmentation, or one can seek to reduce it. Even in high-pressure, high-exposure jobs there are devices for limiting interruptions. Or to put it the other way round, anyone who is crazy enough to work with their door open is inviting drop-ins and distractions. There may be a discretionary element in the amount of travelling. Meetings abroad are seldom an absolute must: mail, telex, facsimile document transmission, and telephone conversations are all substitutes. Or if you really do not want to go, send someone else, someone young enough to think a weekend in Stockholm will be fun.

Or again meetings in general usually offer an element of choice. Even if there are a lot of meetings the manager is officially required to attend there are still techniques for cutting down time spent in meetings. One might send someone else: 'good experience for him, you know, help to bring him out a bit'. If this is not possible one can always miss every third meeting in the series sending in apologies for absence and a plausible excuse. If you are chairing the meeting yourself you can limit the agenda, the duration, or both. Being called out of meetings to take fictitious telephone calls is an old one, but a neater version is being the first to arrive (creates good impression) and announcing you can only stay 40 minutes – play this one right and the chairman will apologise for all you are missing when you leave.

Sometimes management jobs offer the possibility of sharing (some of) the work with, say, same-rank colleagues. This again increases the discretion. You take on X for a colleague, he relieves you of Y, and you have more time for Z. Or you do something together, with complementary strengths, and it becomes easier, or gets done better.

There is always choice, at least for the aware and resourceful.

NOTES

1 In an earlier book I attempted a general characterisation of German management. Peter Lawrence (1980) *Managers and Management in West Germany*, Croom Helm, London. It is a bit dated now, but the stories are good.

2 For an introductory account of company structure supported with a series of real organisation charts see Peter Lawrence and Robert Lee (1984) *Insight into Management*, OUP, Oxford.

3 For a sense of the trend towards more professional purchasing and independent purchasing departments see B. Farrington and M. Woodmansey (1980) *The Purchasing Function*, Management Survey Report No. 50, British Institute of Management, London.

4 These empire-building proclivities of production managers are magnificently and entertainingly portrayed in a short article K.G. Lockyer and Steven Jones (1980) The function factor, *Management Today*, September.

5 Ibid.

6 For this titillating account of power ploys and infighting in a French cigarette factory see Michel Crozier (1964) *The Bureaucratic Phenomenon*, Tavistock Publications, London.

7 This first study of the work of 160 managers is discussed in Rosemary Stewart (1964) *Managers and Their Jobs*, Pan, London.

8 This very sophisticated study of management work patterns is Rosemary Stewart (1976) *Contrasts in Management*, McGraw Hill, Maidenhead.

9 This very clever analysis of areas of choice in management jobs is Rosemary Stewart (1982) *Choices for the Manager*, McGraw Hill, Maidenhead.

4

Management Process or How it is Done

There are a series of plaques let into the wall where the Rue de Rivoli flows into the Place de la Concorde in the centre of Paris and they commemorate young Frenchmen killed in the liberation of August 1944. These plaques speak proudly but vaguely of heroic sacrifice or valiant conduct, except the last which is different. It speaks precisely of a young tank commander from Leclerc's Second Armoured Division who fell but only after having attacked and destroyed a Tiger tank.

What is this inscription celebrating? Not valour, courage, or patriotism – they all have these. It is rather a tribute to purposeful action. Although nothing is won without sacrifice, not all sacrifice wins.

There is a danger in discussing management process that this process is conceived as some woolly interactive flux with things somehow or other being changed at the end. This is not the business we are in. Process is about how things get done, about purposeful action, about admittedly complicated sequences of initiatives and responses but initiatives which are throughout suffused with intentionality. To which should be added the fact that process in this sense is important, is often complex, and its dynamics are not obvious to the uninitiated.

WHERE ARE THE RULES?

Students sometimes suggest by response and posture that it is not really necessary to explore these processes because it is all too straightforward; what happens in any company will simply amount to tracing out the effect of organisational rules and procedures, seeing the company's servants move by process of right reason towards commonly agreed objectives. Perhaps the most cogent, and snappy, rebuttal of this well-meaning innocence is that proferred by Leonard Sayles in his quite magnificent book on leadership.[1] He suggests that there are a number of assumptions or expectations that people newly coming to management hold. Paraphrasing a little these are:

— objectives will be clear
— results will be quick to appear, and clearly associated with inputs of effort (merit rules!)
— there will be plenty of time for analysis and decision-making
— subordinates will respect and respond
— planning is important, and there will be time for it
— means and ends will be clearly defined, and there won't be any contradictions or inconsistencies
— getting promoted will mean fewer people messing around with your decisions
— the resources made available will be equal to the task assigned
— people will be given the necessary authority to carry out their assignments.[2]

The trouble is that most of these assumptions are wrong most of the time. So we need to understand something of process. To begin with something rather basic, how does a manager make his formal authority over subordinates effective? It cannot be taken for granted, it is not enough simply to fill an office with an authority label.[3]

WHAT WILL THEY DO IF I GIVE THEM ORDERS?

The formal answer to the question of how to make authority effective is to say that occupancy of an office designated as carrying authority will so endow the occupant. Not true. It may do no more than generate half-hearted and intermittent compliance, perhaps keeping up authority-appearances when anyone else is around to see, together with an execution of the letter rather than the spirit of instructions. A less formal and more high-minded answer is to say that displaying competence will make authority effective. This is much better as an answer, but it still leaves some things unsaid. What do we mean by competence? The right training, suitable intelligence, appropriate specialised knowledge, and understanding of the work in hand. Yes, all those things, but often they are not enough. Can we not think of people who had all that and yet failed to be effective, to get people to do things. In other words, this notion of competence needs to be enlarged to embrace some understanding of process.

To start at the beginning it helps a new incumbent of an authority position to be 'annointed' by someone else who already enjoys effective authority. It is advantageous, that is, to be brought in as such a person's henchman, right-hand man, natural successor, or chosen instrument of policy; that is a much better start than simply being 'the latest they have sent us from head office'.

In the early days especially, you have to go out and circulate, be available, spread good will. This is difficult, and it goes against one's rational inclinations which suggest that the best thing is to get your head down in the office, read the reports, master the facts, and do it all so well that by the time you do come out you'll be bomb-proof and nobody will be able to ask you a question you cannot answer (doubt your competence). The trouble with this rational approach to establishing authority through competence is that it is a bit like not taking the car on the road until you have passed the driving test. What is more, not all things you need to know are in those reports and computer print-outs, and a lot of what you need will only be got by talking to people (and letting them ask you questions you cannot answer).

There is more to this than simple circulation and availability. You can only influence people with whom you have contact. The new manager's objective is for more than availability; he needs to reduce social distance between himself and people who work for him, to be able to get close to them in an interactive sense. Managers who boast of having an ever open door are only paying lip-service to democracy and equality. What they really want is for people to come and tell them interesting things, especially things other managers don't know. People may also be grateful for and respond to a lowering of social barriers: if their job is not very interesting compared with yours then perhaps talking to you is the most exciting thing they do at work.

In the early stages there is something to be said for getting people to accept orders incrementally. Doing what people tell you is habit forming, just like having a stiff Scotch at six o'clock to celebrate having survived the day. So start with something central and uncontroversial. 'Come and take a letter, Miss Smith' – nobody is going to refuse that. Getting compliance on more peripheral matters is something one can work up to. Compliance may also be affected by example, to ask first the guy most likely to say yes (and it will be incrementally more difficult for the second person to say no).

There are two further related considerations which are absolutely fundamental to effective authority with subordinates, and this in an enduring way not simply as facilitators at 'start up' time. The first is the question of what you do for subordinates and how well you do it. Can you dispense information, provide knowledge based on answers to legitimate questions, use a superior knowledge of procedures or company practice to tell them how to get what they want? Can you adjudicate, have you got the moral courage, the power of decision, and enough authority resources to make it stick when you have decided. But above all, can you solve problems for subordinates, whatever and whenever they are? Can you get them resources, cooperation from other people, sensible decisions from other managers, anything they need to be able to do their jobs?

The second thing overlaps with the first and concerns what was described in the last chapter as Rosemary Stewart's concept of boundary management,[4] the function a manager has of protecting the unit he is in charge of from outside interference, indeed generally stage-managing its relationship with the rest of the organisation. The critical questions are: can you protect subordinates from unreasonable outside demands or undue pressure, get stupid orders from up the line changed, prevent any cuts in resources allocated to your staff, get cooperation and assistance laterally (from equal ranks in other departments over whom you have no control) when your group needs these? Any manager who can solve problems for his staff and manage the boundary in this way is unlikely to have an authority problem.

WHAT ABOUT THE WORKERS?

Suppose the manager's subordinates are ordinary blue-collar workers, does that make a difference, does it enhance the challenge of establishing effective authority? Yes it does. In this case even getting rather literal compliance may be problematic. In the foregoing discussion the implicit reference was to subordinates who were staff specialists, designers or technicians, supervisors or other middle managers; people who have some career stake in the company where one ought to be able to assume a modicum of motivation, of commitment to the work for its own sake. This does not necessarily hold for blue-collar workers.

The challenge is faced in acute form by production managers, but also intermittently by managers from other functions as and when they need to get things done through shop-floor workers. On the basis of experience rather than study three things have struck me as commonly associated with the effective exercise of authority by production managers. The first is practical grasp.

It is often said that workers are not much impressed by formal qualifications and displays of intellectual ability. This is probably true, with a few qualifications about differences from country to country, but it does not mean that workers cannot be impressed. They are indeed quite susceptible to demonstrations of practical prowess: managers who can work the machines themselves, set them up, do repairs that are normally carried out by maintenance people, argue the toss convincingly with inspectors, and advise on do-it-yourself tasks, are away to a head start. I recall a divisional manager in a precision engineering company in Germany telling me that his reputation on the shop floor was based not on his PhD, or on the quite seminal research-based discovery he had made about the physical properties of the company product – a breakthrough which enabled the company to sell the best at the price of the ordinary – but on his ability to re-line motor-car clutches.

Second, production managers have to handle industrial relations issues, and they tend to be much more in the thick of these than personnel managers (an industrial relations problem usually has to reach a certain 'critical mass' to get into the purview of the personnel department). Now there is not any simple formula on how to do this, but one can point to some of the things involved, which all come down to understanding industrial relations as process.[5] The whole thing becomes paradoxically easier when you admit how complicated it is! Industrial relations questions, that is, are generally more complicated than they seem at first sight, and certainly more complicated than media accounts allow. Both sides indeed tend to suppress or at least leave out critical bits of information and circumstantial fact – exactly those which would make it comprehensible to an outsider. When you realise this the thing is simply to dig, and keep on digging until you have all of it, or at least as much as the opposition. In practice it tends to be the workers' representatives rather than the managers who have the superior mastery of the facts (they have less to worry about of course), but it is an imbalance which can be corrected with patience.

Another important part of the ability to cope with industrial relations issues is recognising some of the political-tactical angles. Things such as the fact that a generalised grievance may give rise to particular but not directly connected complaints. If long-term overtime working has been withdrawn, for example, this may make for a general feeling of deprivation which gives rise to complaints about safety or working conditions. Indeed bringing together for bargaining purposes things not actually connected is a common tactic employed against management, who often react as though appalled by the irrationality of such a move (though it is the second time they have been caught this week). So that, for instance, management asks for a new working practice to be accepted and workers respond by asking for a bigger car park, less sub-contracting, or every third Friday afternoon off.

Industrial relations issues are sometimes raised for purely tactical reasons, not with any expectation of winning. Perhaps a shop steward simply wants to show management he has not gone to sleep, or impress on his 'constituents' that no case is too arduous for his amazing advocacy. Or maybe he aims to lose, perhaps to lose three in a row, to be able to say on a more viable issue next week: 'I can't keep going back to the men empty handed.'

Third, the most successful production managers I have known have been ones with an abundance of social skills. The point is also laboured in an excellent discussion by Leonard Sayles who says that what managers need in this context is 'interactive energy', an endless ability to be with, talk to, and have exchanges with subordinates.[6] Sayles develops the idea saying that this interaction, to be effective, has to be frequent, and evenly distributed among subordinates. It is not enough to have half-hour chats with the two or three you find easiest to talk to, indeed this might be counter-productive. The interaction also involves much sensitivity on the manager's side and the ability to be flexible as to duration and synchronisation. Again it would be counter-productive for the manager with his greater self-confidence and probably higher educational standing to overwhelm or engulf subordinates; the need is to match the exchange in a variable way.

It is not suggested that these three things – practical prowess, industrial relations capability, and the famous interactive energy – are total answers to all questions of worker motivation and performance; but they certainly take many managers a long way.

SIDEWAYS TO THE FINISHING POST

The management literature tends to neglect the lateral relationships. Of course a manager's relations with boss and subordinates are important, but for many managers these sideways relationships with equal-rank managers in other departments predominate, and diagonal relationships with the superiors and subordinates of these managers as a variation on the theme. The last chapter showed how the production manager, for example, is connected with or dependent on a range of people in other departments or sections including design, production engineering, production control, maintenance, quality control, and sales. Or again the output of personnel and finance departments affects everyone in the company, and there is a lot of interdepartmental contact.

Specialists in management services departments may be working for any department in the company, and are probably in dialogue with several at any given time, to build up their range of potential customers. Purchasing managers variously liaise with design, engineering, and production, and sometimes with finance. Sales and marketing are often in contact with R&D or design, about what the customer would or will like, with production about what the customer is going to get, with production control about when the customer is going to get it, with quality control about how good it is going to be, and with finance about the credit terms the customer will enjoy. And so it goes on, not to mention lateral/diagonal semi-external contacts with other works in the group, sister factories, sales offices abroad, R&D establishments somewhere else, and head office (which head office, the one in London, the one in Hamburg, or the one in New Jersey?).

One might express it another way by raising the question, in all these lateral relationships, what actually does the manager seek? It is a range of things. Sometimes it is pure information, but it may be information that is not instantly available so perhaps the manager asking has to exert powers of persuasion or whatever to get his interlocutor to spend the time and take the trouble to put the information together. On the other hand, it may not be information so much as a favourable decision – about anything. Perhaps a decision about work loads, or delivery dates, or costs, or priorities, or about levels of service from one department to another, or about procedures or conventions, or about some complex act of coordination. Or it maybe that the initiator wants to be granted something, more time, more money, more resources of some other kind, permission to violate some established procedure, or commitment to a new policy. Or perhaps the initiator wants support: moral support, tactical support, political support to get something, to overturn a restrictive decision, to have something changed for the better, to get promoted or someone else promoted, to rearrange some bit of the organisational structure of the who-reports-to-whom kind, to fix the terms of reference of an investigating committee, to alter the mission of a task force, to establish a fall-back position in case things go wrong.

Or again perhaps the initiator wants to be exonerated; he has fouled-up something and wants to be forgiven, put another manager or another department in a difficult position and wants to square it, to make amends. The initiator is, say, a salesman who has told a customer they can have in 6 weeks something which takes 8 weeks to make; he is an engineer telling the purchasing officer they must buy some component from a particular supplier because the engineer was chatted into giving a commitment to the supplier (that he is, strictly speaking, not allowed to give); he is a production manager going to finance to tell them a junior manager dispatched completed work to customers without informing finance who in consequence have not invoiced the customers. In short, there are a lot of contingencies, a lot of issues which bring managers in different functions into contact. The broad question is, how does one make a success of these contacts, how does one run lateral relationships where one has no authority over those one is dealing with?

As with relationships with workers there is no guaranteed formula, but one can certainly point to certain things which the more successful practitioners have going for them. There are no prizes for guessing that the first is Sayles' interactive energy again. Perhaps more properly, a social repertoire ranging from casual cheerfulness through human sympathy to charismatic impact! It is not just a case of agreeableness or persuasiveness 'at the point of sale', when favours are sought, when bargains are struck, but of sustaining middle-term relationships.

At the same time lateral relationships generally have to be fuelled with more than interactive energy. They are frequently 'trading relationships' where both sides give something. This will not be obvious to outsiders where the exchange is not something officially ordained. Or to put it the other way round, in many cases a relationship will appear to be asymetrical: B needs cooperation from A but has nothing to give in return. The trick is to work out what A could possibly need that you have to give: when you have done it, you have a trading relationship, and can trade on it. An example may help here.

Consider the plight of the purchasing officer.[7] He likes to have freedom to shop around, compare the terms and offers of rival suppliers, do fantastic deals with beautiful discounts and wonderful credit arrangements, in general to show his virtuosity. But supposing the design engineers, the people who obviously know better than anyone what kind of components are needed for the product they have designed, specify these components in too fine a detail. The effect may be to narrow the purchasing officer's choice, perhaps to the extent that there is only one viable supplier. This takes the fun out of his job, reduces him to an order-placing clerk, but what can he bargain with to get the design engineer to loosen up the specifications?

The best tactic is probably to sit quiet for a bit. Designers and engineers are not perfect, they forget things occasionally, make mistakes, even get caught being taken out to dinner by the supplier's salesman. So sooner or later they will need a favour, a wrong order changed, an order for components that was placed too late speeded up by the purchasing officer using his personal pull with the supplier, an illicit dinner party conveniently forgotten, an alternative supplier found at short notice, a more flexible credit arrangement established to the benefit of the design department's budget, or whatever. Sevices which must be worth something in return.

Outsiders would probably be surprised at the extent to which managers do favours and build up commitments almost as a matter of policy, so that they have some chips to call in when they need to. Production managers are the exponents *par excellence* of this tactic. Being heavily dependent on a range of other functions, the laterally astute production manager loses no opportunities to help his fellow man, show sympathy and understanding, forgive the errors of others, even help to conceal them. Next week his head may be on the block.

Another thing which is not obvious is that it is not only favours and reciprocities of service that are traded, so is information. Not formal information that one can get on a VDU screen or from last year's company report, but hot-information, information other managers do not have yet, the real reasons, the inside story, what the boss thinks, who is going to run the new sales subsidiary, gossip which happens to be right.

Not only is the information often of real value to the receiver, who wants to know the current threats and opportunities, and which of his war aims to pursue, but there may also be psychological gratifications. It is nice to be in the know, to have the latest gen, to be able to tell (trade with) other people, to be the confident of the really high-powered guy from R&D who knows what head office are thinking before they have even thought it.

Finally there are threats, though they have to be used sparingly. The trouble with threatening people is that they may call your bluff and then you have to climb down or see it through and both alternatives are usually embarrassing. A manager resorting to threats may well find it more effective to threaten indirectly, to construe the threat as an impersonal happening which may somehow overtake them both: 'It would be much better for us to find a way to settle this amicably, we'll both look a bit silly if we have to call in the technical director'; or 'If you don't give me the help I need my section's performance will be so bad that the whole story is likely to come out at the annual performance review.'

GAINING POWER IN THE ORGANISATION

How does one enlarge one's influence and area of operations in the company? There are indeed some definable strategies to achieve this glorious end.[8] How viable they are will depend on the particular circumstances of individual managers as well as on an understanding of process, but some of them will work some of the time.

First of all avoid routinisation of the work activity. The trouble with routine is that there is no credit for getting it right but plenty of blame for getting it wrong. And there are other angles. If the work is routinised then by definition it does not require an especially gifted person to run it. What is more the routine will be rather visible to outsiders (managers from other departments); they will be able to look at your operation, understand it all too easily, and tell you how to handle it – in order to accommodate their outlandish requests, perhaps. The fact that the work is a routine will also mean that others can calculate the results, so the operation becomes dependable and predictable, so no one will need to come to you for assurances: that won't inaugurate many trading relationships.

On the other hand one does seek control of critical operations. A critical operation is one that is important, that other people depend on, where your discretionary competence is difficult for others to control. Ideally, from the standpoint of the power-developing manager, a critical function is one which no one else (no othe unit) can perform, which everyone needs, and which is, or can be plausibly depicted as being, very difficult to routinise. In the last chapter we referred to Michel Crozier's study of a cigarette factory in France where the maintence fitters were in just this position of a discretionary service needed by many, a position which they shamelessly exploited.[9] In industry any post which has to do with the allocation of resources has something of this character, whatever the resources concerned. Or again so do many of the 'money jobs' – determining budgets, monitoring the performance of units in financial terms, allocating costs or overheads between various sections, setting internal transfer prices (the cost of something made by one part of the works and supplied to another), putting a cost figure on services such as maintenance or use of computer time by various departments, and so on.

Next, it may be possible for the manager to raise the status of his department, perhaps by professionalising the work. This might involve taking on more difficult assignments, raising standards, extending the process, taking on better qualified staff to do these things or securing training and perhaps upward regradings for existing staff. Such developments should be accompanied by 'throwing away' the routine bits! Another good move in this connection is any additions which would reduce dependence on other departments or functions. Things like a section having its own transport, or its own computer, or its own maintenance service, its own purchasing unit, or an acknowledged right to deal directly with head office or customers or a government department without 'going through channels'.

A very good manoeuvre for increasing sectional power is what is called 'moving up the decision chain'. The idea is to be involved in decision processes at an earlier rather than later stage – which gives more information, more control, and more options.

The difficulty is finding a way in, finding a way to convince a superior or another department whose business the decision really is that you have a plausible reason for being involved. A good tactic here may be humility crossed with helpfulness: 'Although we could not possibly conduct this selection exercise on our own, Mr Personnel Manager, if one of our people could sit in on those first interviews you give to applicants we might be able to save you a bit of time by ruling out candidates whose purely technical qualifications are not quite what we are looking for' (personnel can do the donkey work and we will make the decisions).

To these strategies of de-routinisation, critical-skills acquisition, and sectional-status raising, the idea of innovation should be added. A section which undertakes innovation raises its visibility and status. If the episode of innovation is successful then any extra resources that the section demanded have now been justified, they can demand more resources in the future with greater confidence, the manager in charge of the section will be further along the learning curve of how to implement change than his colleagues in other sections, and will be well placed to pre-emptively volunteer for any new episode of corporate change which comes along and will be status-enhancing for the unit that executes it.

Finally in this connection of gaining power in the organisation there is a residuum of illicit power ploys. These include devices such as restricting the access of others to information, releasing incomplete information, declining to give explanations to others which would allow them to exercise some control, playing off against each other competing demands for service, and even restricting access to senior people.

ADVOCACY

Pervading all the processes discussed – making authority effective, handling subordinates, making a success of lateral relationships, seeking to enhance power in the organisation – is a particular ability, the power of advocacy. The ability to plead, to make the case, is all important, whether it is done on paper, in open meetings, or fact to face with individual seniors. Time and again the manager will want things – more resources, more cooperation, more support, more time, advantages at the expense of other managers and departments, and these will only be obtainable by a cogent presentation of the case.

What is more the act of advocacy itself has to be good, and cannot usually be circumvented by back-room work or politicing. It makes sense for a manager to set up allies for the project he wishes to advocate, to 'fix the meeting', plant favourable ideas concerning the intended initiative, do his homework and marshal facts, but having done all this the critical document will have to be drafted or the issue persuasively argued in some competitive forum. The ability to engage in effective advocacy is no simple correlate of intelligence or educational level.

STUDYING PROCESS

Management process in the sense of this chapter is not a subject that one ever knows 'all about', though it can be variously apprehended by analysis and experience. There are, I suspect, strategic sites for its observation and study, particularly the adversarial situations in management. Industrial relations are one such case, already explored in this chapter in connection with the question of making authority effective. A similar at least quasi-adversarial quality often pervades the relationship between individual plants and head office, with information and control initiatives from the latter being diluted, perverted, and resisted by the former.[10]

Another situation which lends itself to the study of process is the presence of outside consultants in a company.[11] Their presence is generally (and rightly) seen as a threat by those departments under investigation, who are at pains to protect themselves from serious criticism and above all rationalisation (rationalisation is seldom good news).

BIAS OR BASIS?

It would be fair to say that there are two biases in the foregoing account. The first is that in this chapter the implicit reference has been to managers in the more exposed and interactive line jobs, the chief executive-general manager–production manager line, designated in the previous chapter in explaining the gap between the Carlson–Mintzberg–Lawrence findings on management activity and the more qualified and heterogeneous picture to emerge from the research studies of Rosemary Stewart.

The second bias is that I have (jocularly) overplayed the political nature of management process, not to distort or deceive but to help get the ideas across. Neither of these biases, however, is invalidating. It is only the degree not the fact which is exaggerated, and all management jobs partake of these processes even if some are more exposed than others.

This leads to a last question, often put by students, which amounts to asking, why is it like this? Why, that is, is a static and formal account of management quite inadequate, why is it necessary to resort to analyses of activity and process to understand what is going on and how things get done? Why in fact are the assumptions of the neophyte manager as formulated by Leonard Sayles and presented at the start of this chapter in fact wrong?

WHY IS THE WORLD LIKE THIS?

One perfectly legitimate response is to turn the question on its head and ask why not? In other words it is quite reasonable to argue that the essence of management is dealing with the unexpected, the routine being able to take care of itself. Or to put it another way, management is a contingency activity, it is about coping with things that 'crop up' and which may 'foul-up' the system unless dealt with. If one accepts this starting point then the reasons for the relative absence of planning, rational decision-making, systematic data gathering, and powerful analysis becoming all too clear.

It is also right to reinstate the human nature of management. It is not a machine, but a human entity. And most of these humans have a general predilection for other humans as sources of information, inspiration, and support. They want to be told things, see for themselves, talk through ideas and solutions, not get them from mathematical models or computer print-outs. It is the same with decisions: the premium is not on perfectly rational decisions, but on acceptable decisions; on decisions worked out by human problem solvers and acceptable to them notwithstanding the range of special interests. It is, in other words, the literal humanness of management that makes process, in our sense, important.

All this is very much reinforced by the business context. Because companies aim to make a profit they aim to keep costs down; so there are never enough resources to go round, and there is always competition for these resources among managers. What is more this resource oriented competition seems natural to those who establish and run businesses, since competition is germane to the free enterprise system and the natural state of inter-company relations. It is but a short step from here to the belief, generally current, that competition within companies is healthy and desirable – between managers, ideas, and projects. These convictions, of course, put a premium on understanding process.

Harold Leavitt of Stanford has offered a formulation which parallels this argument.[12] His view is that business leadership involves three elements: pathfinding, decision-making, implementation. Pathfinding is an intuitive act, decision-making alone is in principle rational, and implementation Leavitt describes as idiosyncratic. In other words, there are no rules for implementation (or for pathfinding for that matter), it is a question of squaring it with interested parties, negotiating acceptance, finding out by trial and error what will work. And implementation, of course, is what managers do most of. Their work is process.[13]

NOTES

1 Leonard R. Sayles (1979) *Leadership: What Effective Managers Really Do and How They Do It*, McGraw Hill Book Company, New York.

2 My rendering of the list of false expectations that newly appointed managers have from Sayles, op. cit.

3 Again a lot of these ideas in this ensuing discussion of how to make authority effective are taken from Sayles, op. cit.

4 For this concept of boundary management see Rosemary Stewart (1982) *Choices for the Manager*, McGraw Hill

Book Company, London. This concept is also discussed in the last section of chapter 3.

5 A more detailed account of the dynamics of industrial relations process is offered in Peter Lawrence (1984) *Management in Action*, Routledge & Kegan Paul, London.

6 For a discussion of the importance of interactive energy see Sayles op. cit.

7 This example is inspired by: G. Strauss (1962) Tactics of lateral relationships: the purchasing agent, *Administrative Science Quarterly*, no. 7, September.

8 Again I have taken many of these ideas on enlarging one's power and influence in the organisation from Sayles, op. cit.

9 Michel Crozier (1963) *The Bureaucratic Phenomenon*, Tavistock Publications, London.

10 For a more detailed discussion with practical examples of the head office–works relationship see Peter Lawrence (1984) *Management in Action*, Routledge & Kegan Paul, London.

11 For a really jolly account of how the managers *in situ* may resist the unwelcome intentions of outside consultants see: David Clutterbuck (1982) How to survive an external consultant, *International Management*, March.

12 This view of Leavitt that management consists of pathfinding, decision-making, and implementation is quoted and discussed in: Thomas J. Peters and Robert H. Waterman Jr. (1982) *In Search of Excellence*, Harper & Row, New York.

13 If you have found this chapter fun and want to read something else that treats management process as a power game, and offers practical tips on how to win, you will probably enjoy: Bob Lee and Peter Lawrence (1985) *Organisational Behaviour: Politics at Work*, Hutchinson, London.

5

Small is Beautiful

Books about management are usually about management in big corporations, at least implicitly. There is some justification for this because the little company, run by its founder, is a very different affair, and a lot of the conventional management wisdom does not apply. Neither is there very much career overlap. Able and ambitious people go to university, study business subjects, and spend their lives working for big companies; it is mostly other people, who generally do not go to university, who found new companies and run them. This is the way things have been but it is changing.

The recession of the 1980s, and the unemployment problem, have been accompanied by an increase in the rate of new business formation. What is more quasi-new business formation in the sense of management buyouts[1] and franchising,[2] have also increased, the latter on a massive scale. More jobs have been created in the small-business sector than by established concerns, more courses on business start-ups are on offer, sometimes as options on university management degree courses, and the encouragement of the small-firms sector is official policy in most Western countries. Even banks are adapting lending practices to the needs of would-be entrepreneurs and battling small-firm owners, at least they say so.

So what is a small company like, what is involved in running one? There is a famous exchange between two expatriate American writers in Paris in the 1920s on the subject of what it means to be rich: 'The rich are different from us,' asserted Scott Fitzgerald; 'Yes,' countered Ernest Hemingway, 'they have more money.'

There is a tendency to assume that Hemingway won this exchange, a triumph of robust middle-western common sense over east-coast romanticism. But perhaps Fitzgerald has a point. Maybe differences in wealth imply differences in style, experience of life, expectations, and consciousness; differences, that is, of a qualitative kind that go beyond the dollars-per-head gap. It is arguable that the same kind of difference emerges when one seeks to characterise small businesses. They are not 'just like' big companies only smaller. They are qualitatively different and inhabit a differently structured environment.

To start with the small company has no chequer board of different departments and functions. There is no sales as distinct from finance, and purchasing as distinct from production; normally all managerial functions are discharged by the owner-manager. Only in the case of partnerships is there likely to be sharing of management functions, some degree of specialisation, as between two or three people. But commonly the owner-manager is alone.

Not only is the owner-manager obliged to be competent in all management functions in the way described above, there is usually little scope for delegation. In practice owner-managers may delegate office routine, production supervision, distribution in the homely sense of putting things in a van and taking them to customers, routine order taking, and not very much else. To put it positively the owner-manager will make all the money decisions, do the buying and selling, be responsible for what in the language of big companies is called manufacturing and business policy, and settle all personnel questions.

This is a good deal. It calls for some versatility. It also involves some traps for people starting their own company. A common one is that the would-be entrepreneur whose impulse comes from invention, one who has created something people might want to buy and figured out how to make it, has to sell it as well. Selling requires different skills, and a lot of people who start companies do not have any experience of selling. Another is that those who start companies and have not run a business before, though a surprising number are 'second-time buyers', do not know how to handle the money questions – where to get it, how to count the money, and how to do without it.

There are other senses in which the owner-managed firm is 'existentially squeezed' compared with its 'big brothers', the large companies. Big companies usually have a past, a substantial past, and the normal expectation is that they have an extended future as well. They fill a substantial amount of space as well as time, they are an economic and geographically identifiable presence. Not only do they have functional specialisation, they have graded hierarchies of managers, controlled information systems, and organisationally contrived ways of seeing the wood from the trees.

Little of this applies to small firms. Many have no past, the future is questionable, and they are but pimples on the economic landscape. The owner-manager is bombarded by a *mélange* of the important and trivial without any formal mechanism for sifting them, or passing them upwards, downwards, or sideways.

FORTUNE'S WHEEL

The small firm is much more affected by chance. It is much more likely that some little thing turns out to be important. Positively speaking a lucky break has more far-reaching consequences; negatively, it does not take much to knock a small firm off balance. The breaks are difficult to predict and programme, though one can see them when they happen; there is, however, some patterning of the characteristic problems.

To take a simple thing small companies often move, change premises. Many are started in private houses, garages, or back-bedrooms, perhaps as a spare-time supplementary activity while the would-be entrepreneur is holding down a normal job. At the point where he or she gives up this job, however, a move to separate or purpose-built premises is usual. If a small business succeeds a further move to larger and better premises may be not just desirable but essential. Where the business prospers the expanded manufacturing facility and workers to man it may necessitate larger premises. Or again the numerous business competitions that have blossomed in the 1980s often require the winners to move into the geographic area of the organiser-sponsor in the expectation of benefiting that area with new jobs.

It may seem a small consideration but just think of the disruption entailed by a physical move. The production of goods or services stops for days, the office routine is disrupted, and there will be a setting-up cum sorting-out phase at the new premises, however desirable they may be. Note that big companies do not move. They close uneconomic plants, open new plants, and add on bits, but they hardly ever have to pick up the whole works and move it somewhere else.

Small firms again are often at loggerheads with the municipal authorities in whose area they locate. The small firm is really dreadfully vulnerable in this respect. It is often scruffy enough to attract local government attention, and may well be sailing close to the wind with regard to local by-laws, safety rules, and environmental legislation. At the same time, unlike the big company, it does not have any clout, it cannot bite back, so that it is generally vulnerable to interference and even malpractice by others.

Small firms often have an acute need for ready money. In this they are not alone. Some big companies live on credit to an extent which would horrify the general public, but at least they can get credit in normal times, and there is even competition to lend to them. This need for ready money inclines the owner-managers of small firms to do a variety of things. One of the commonest is debt-factoring. This is where the small firm supplies a customer with goods or services but instead of waiting for payment passes the collecting of the money from the customer to a third party in return for an agreed portion of the debt paid on the spot. In other words the firm gets less, but it gets it straight away.

Like many things which small firms do it is good for short-term cash flow but bad for the middle-term profitability. In the same way it is not unusual for small firms to use middlemen, some extra and arguably unnecessary link in the distributive system, simply because the middleman can pay (less) now, or take on the holding costs of waiting to find customers, or waiting to get money out of them. Again in the interests of getting money quickly it is not unknown for the small business owner to make the deliveries personally, be his own truck driver, in the hope of bringing back a few cheques as well as delivery receipts.

Because of the small businessman's double problem, finding start-up capital and managing the business's cash flow, there is a premium on finding ways of doing without money. It is not an impossibility, there are ways.

DOING IT WITHOUT MONEY

To start with a quite straightforward dodge, some businessmen operate, or at least get started, by factoring on trade credit. When the business owner buys something from other manufacturers he does not usually have to pay for it straight away. There is probably a requirement to pay in 30 or 60 days, or some more complicated variation thereon such as having to pay by the end of the following month if delivered before the 15th of the present month. Now suppose our businessman wants these things he has bought not as raw materials, not so much as inputs to his own manufacturing process, but to re-sell them, say in smaller lots, or better packaged, or with some assembly work done first, then it may be possible to do all this within the credit period. To assemble (or whatever), re-sell, and collect before payment to the supplier falls due. This is factoring on trade credit. At least in theory it is possible to do this with no start-up capital and no working capital.

There are some other stratagems that minimise the need for money, and they have a common thread. This is the realisation that a business is based on an idea. The idea will be how to make better, or more cheaply, or more interestingly, something that people will pay for, even imagining a product or service which does not exist yet that could find buyers. But it is the idea which is paramount, not the production and still less owning the means of production. In other words you do not have to do the making yourself, or all of the making, or execute all the stages of production or service provision. It may be possible to subcontract these, to pay others or other companies to do these things. In so far as this is possible it saves having to spend money on plant, machinery, and stocks of materials, and may reduce the need for employees.

A variation on this theme is that it may be possible to organise the provision of the service or manufacture of the product by outworkers, labouring in their own homes (net-working is the up-market word for it). If the whole business can be organised in this way the cost of premises is completely obviated, and so are some of the indirect costs of having a workforce (you do not have to provide them with loos, canteens, or car-parking lots). Obviously the outworker solution is not always applicable: it does not work for fork-lift trucks but it will work for much of the toy industry. It is important not to dismiss the option too blithely. It may have connotations of the eighteenth-century textile industry, but that has not stopped the later twentieth-century computer software houses getting a lot of mileage out of it. Or again publishers have for decades delegated substantial elements of the editorial process – copy-editing, proof-reading, sometimes index compilation – to outworkers.

Working out of domestic premises, of course, eliminates the need to pay for industrial or commercial premises, though there are limitations. Leasing, both of premises or equipment, may reduce the need for capital at the outset. In particular the leasing of plant and machinery has become much more common and is often supported by ready-made financial packages devised by the lessor and bank in cooperation. It all helps to avoid having to find large sums up front, and having money tied up in equipment, for which there may be a better business use.

In the same connection small companies and especially new

companies have a need for credibility. They need to impress all sorts of people – banks, suppliers, creditors, potential customers, 'the trade' generally – in both nebulous and particular ways. The small firm wants to be perceived as sound, consequential, and above all 'here to stay'. Big companies in part achieve this effect by the size and style of their premises, especially their head offices. The Nestlé headquarters on the north side of Lake Geneva, Schering AG rising glittering above the drabness of Wedding in West Berlin, the STC building at the top of the Strand in London are all good examples – and cost millions. How can small firms fabricate big-firm status on a shoestring? An example may help.

A company that I know began life more or less factoring on trade credit. The owner-manager had one employee only, a secretary, and the company was located in one room over a shop. Not a particularly good hand to play if you want to pretend to be General Motors! But incoming orders came by telephone, and the phone was answered by the secretary. No one ever saw the premises, and in the early days this owner made a point of not having any local customers so that no one would be likely to visit his office. What the customers and for that matter suppliers saw was a personable owner visiting customers in his car, a telephone that was always manned, and immaculate paperwork – letterheads, 'with compliments' slips, invoices, quotation forms, all suggestive of the large, well-run company. As a final touch this owner had deliveries to customers made by Securicor, a private high-speed delivery service (this last was a lucky break, the owner having a business friend who had already contracted more Securicor capacity than he actually needed and was selling-off cheap). When this entrepreneur won a business competiton and moved to a new industrial unit as part of the prize settlement, he consented to sell locally and receive visitors.[3]

REACHING A MARKET

Most small firms probably start with the idea of a product or a service. In the entrepreneur's mind the emphasis is usually on how to make the product or organise the provision of the service. For many not only the act of selling, but defining the market, and measures for getting at it, are at one remove. The point to emphasise is that it is not all common sense. Defining markets, especially where a new product is concerned, is often difficult. It also poses a need for information, perhaps information which the entrepreneur does not have and cannot easily get.

At the outset an entrepreneur may want to know how big a market is: quite simply how many people, organisations, or institutions are there that might want to buy the thing he is about to make. Imagine, for example, that I design a little personal trolley that people might use to cart things around on. My first thought is that it will be useful to anglers who can put fishing tackle on it. Fine, how many anglers are there? No one knows, it is not something on which the national statistical office is likely to keep figures. How do you get at anglers? Through shops that sell fishing tackle of course. Fine, but these are usually small independent retailers, not organised into chains as is, say, the grocery trade, so there is no head office or central purchasing unit. I can only get at retailers of fishing tackle by tramping the country and calling on them. Not inconceivable, things are sold in this way, but I am a small firm, there is only one of me, and I cannot send my few production workers out on the road or delegate management decisions to them while I am away.

My next thought is that anglers are not the only possibility. My product is equally useful to shoppers, golfers, campers, and picknickers. But again I do not know the numbers, so I cannot calculate how much I would make in the first year of business if I managed to sell to one out of every ten in the various categories of potential user. And how do I go about getting to them? It is not that there are no known methods, but rather that one does not know which method is most appropriate or will be most cost-effective. Shall I for instance go for selling to retail chains, general promotional advertising, advertising in special-interest publications of the *Angling News* type, or perhaps door-to-door calling or 'mailingshotting' (sending out descriptions of the goods or service through the post) would be more productive. And what should I concentrate on, since it is going to be difficult to pursue all these openings: does my middle-term interest lie with aging anglers, gouty golfers, or supermarket freaks?

All this is much easier for big companies. They have done it before, and even if it is a question of a completely new product they at least have a system in place. They have salesmen already, and service centres, and a market research unit, and perhaps long-term dealings with an advertising agency. What is more, if they do not at first succeed in launching a new product they can usually keep on 'throwing money at it' until the results start to come in. Our small firm owner, on the other hand, may spend £1000 on advertising and if that does not bring in commensurate orders he may well be unable to finance repeat onslaughts on the dormant market.

That in general terms is the sort of problem faced by the incipient small-business manager. Is there an answer? There are two. The first, quite simply, is being aware of the problem. Many people who set up small firms are only dimly aware of it, not because they are naturally thoughtless but because they are thinking (and worrying) about other things – where to get the money, how to find the premises, pay for the equipment, oganise production, and so on. In a lot of cases it is possible to think it through before going into action, to do some amateur market research, to try to test-sell the idea to a few representative people whether they be professional purchasing officers for other companies, independent retailers, or members of the general public. The second answer is that there is a standard tactic for small firms entering the business world and this is to locate and develop a market niche.

THE MARKET NICHE IDEA

A niche is a gap in the market which one company can fill better than anyone else. It is based on a distinctive competence of some kind. Perhaps the small firm makes or provides something that no other firm does. If fills a niche, and there is no competition, at least until others see that there is money to be made here and enter the market.

To take a simple example, I know of a company where the owner invented a trailer-parker system. It is a post to which caravans can be hitched, which makes it impossible to steal them. So far as this entrepreneur knows no other company in Britain makes these theft-proof parking posts. So he has no opposition to fight, he must simply sell the idea of security posts to a range of first-time buyers.

Or the niche may be created by design flair. Take wind-powered generators (generators with windmills on top!). The practical difficulty with these is that actually quite strong wind is needed to overcome the inertia and get the windmill turning; this resistance to initial motion is called stiction or cogging. The proprietor of a small firm I know has designed a superior wind-powered generator which has reduced this stiction quite significantly. The result: he has a functionally superior product with no competition worth mentioning.

Sometimes the niche is a particular location on the quality spectrum. Again I know the owner of a small business which produces ornamental Christmas stockings. There is competition, but these particular Christmas stockings are simply very appealing, well executed, designs. If the proprietress tried to sell them to High Street shops she might fail, but in selling them to the best London departmental stores she succeeds very well. She is exploiting a quality niche.

Another possibility is that the niche may be the result of a new application of an existing process or material. There is, for instance, a successful company which has seen the possibility of using holographs (three-dimensional images composed of light) for advertising purposes. Customers, that is, may commission the design and production of holographs which depict their products. The principles of holography are well established in theoretical physics, and there are other applications, but this company alone has exploited holography for the purpose of emblematic advertising.

Or again the niche may be provided by a gap in the distribution system. Perhaps a certain kind of customer/user is not being catered for, perhaps customers in a particular area are neglected, or perhaps it is a case of something being equally available to everyone (all potential customers) but there are *times* when it is not available. Consider as an example a small company I know which deals in nickel cadmium batteries (they are rechargeable power sources). Now the makers of these batteries are big companies and they manufacture on a large scale. Their interest is production not distribution. They are ready, of course, to sell in volume to stockists or other large buyers, but are not interested in selling in small amounts to a variety of end-users. Furthermore these batteries come in all shapes and sizes, and end-users usually need them to be assembled in variable combinations. The small company in this case buys in bulk from large manufacturers, assembles battery packs for all sorts of end-users, and on-sells to them. This small business is not in competition with the large manufacturers, indeed they are pleased to have it offer the service it does to their ultimate customers and provide it with many of its sales leads.

Now market-niche theory admittedly does not tell an entrepreneur how to reach a market, but it at least defines a market in relation to the distinctive competence-based business. The niche offers two further advantages to small companies. In practice servicing the niche often means customised, discriminating operations, getting small things right for the discerning. Small firms are good at this. Their smallness renders them more flexible, and the better able to offer a personal service that will be perceived as such. The other advantage is that finding a suitable niche may obviate competition, especially competiton with bigger and stronger companies, as for instance in the case of the company dealing in rechargeable batteries described above. In other words the niche strategy offers the small firm the possibility of 'peaceful co-existence' in the economic world.

EDUCATION AND ENTREPRENEURSHIP

Are success in starting a business enterprise and education connected? The evidence does not provide a clear-cut answer; it all depends what kind of business, and what is meant by education. It would seem that education, especially higher education, must confer a variety of advantages. Apart from gerneral knowledge and perhaps relevant specialist knowledge as well, there is enhanced reasoning ability, analytical skills, and greater self-confidence, together with larger range of social experience and contacts.

At first sight it would seem that these presumptions are justified by the evidence from studies correlating business formation success with educational level. Yet if one probes further it emerges that the advantage conferred by higher education is not evenly distributed across the spectrum of business operations, but applies to businesses in the manufacturing rather than service sector. What is more, it seems to operate in the high-technology areas in particular. In other words, this finding of a positive association between higher education and business success is probably being produced by the business endeavours of science, engineering, and computer studies graduates in such areas as electronics, computers, software, and instrument engineering.

If, however, one broadens the concept of education to include learning by doing then the whole picture changes in that it is frequently occupational experience as an employee which provides the insight into a business area. By working in a certain business one acquires knowledge of products, ways of making them, an understanding of the market, possible contacts with customers, and general trade knowledge. The type of business one founds is very heavily conditioned by one's previous occupational experience.[4] It is shop-assistants who become shopkeepers, cooks who become restaurant proprietors, computer programmers who found software houses.

When we put these two ideas together – the advantages of education and prior occupational experience as an entrepreneurial entry qualification – the result is a poignant message for the well-educated. No doubt there are many areas in which they could do well as entrepreneurs, often better than the people who typically enter them, yet the way the education system works means they miss the experience-based entry qualification for most of them, the high-technology areas being an obvious exception. This is at least a strong implicit plea for blending work experience and higher education.

NOTES

1 A management buy-out is where managers employed by a company buy it, or a part of it, and then run it as owner-managers. The situation commonly arises as an alternative to the liquidation of the existing company, or the existing company's desire to sell off part of the company, a part it judges to be doing badly, to have poor business prospects, or sometimes simply to have become estranged from the company's main business.

2 A franchise operation is where the franchisor offers participation in a business idea, an established format, and operational know-how, typically accompanied by the benefits of nation-wide advertising, while the franchisee puts up capital and puts in hard work; both share the profits of the operation according to an agreed formula.

3 This and other examples of resourcefulness by small firm entrepreneurs are discussed in Peter Lawrence *et al.* (1985) *Small Business Breakthrough*, Basil Blackwell, Oxford.

4 This idea of a strong association between prior occupational experience and the later area of entrepreneurial endeavour is discussed in Peter Lawrence *et al.*, op. cit.

6

Foreign Affairs

An American friend told of a business trip to South Korea he made with a colleague that got away to a bad start. Their aeroplane was diverted, and they were bused a long way across country in heavy rain. The evening already advanced, they met their host-contact in Seoul who asked hospitably if they were hungry. 'A little bit, may be,' they replied, which is polite American for, 'we're bushed, so how about a quick hamburger and we'll go to bed at ten.' Their host was delighted with this display of coyness, and drove them to a good hotel in downtown Seoul; inside, and then down a staircase to a private room. In the centre a round table, set for a meal of some standing and around the table a circular couch in plush velvet with silken scatter cushions. The air was perfumed. By now the host feels he has mastered the American code. The visitors request for beer to drink with the meal is dismissed as a well-meant but unnecessary move to save expense. Their second choice of wine is clearly no more than a ritual denial of manliness, a quaint deferring to the prowess of the host, who accordingly ordered them a bottle of whisky each. At this point the three girls came in.

* * *

Managers are going abroad more and more in connection with their work, on trips and for foreign placements. The point about abroad is that it is different from the place at which the traveller starts. Because it is different, there are things to learn about it, operating challenges, things you cannot do, as well as unscheduled opportunities. Outcomes are often the product of these differences, some resolution of the gap between wants and expectations on the two sides, but this is not without dangers. Most awkward for the manager abroad are those situations where expectations about both social behaviour and private morals clash, as in the case above.

How do they become exposed to these risks and opportunities? Above all else it is through selling, and this is where we will start but with a backward look at the sales function in the home country.

SALES REVISITED

In the earlier discussion of sales the emphasis was on the variability of the sales operation, but in the present connection it will probably be more helpful to start by distinguishing between sales and marketing. The difficulty is that marketing is an idea, a totality, and a euphemism, and the three sometimes get confused.

Marketing as an idea is undoubtedly an American inspiration. Its essence is that the customer is king, that companies succeed by producing goods or services that customers will buy. The implied or excluded contrast is that companies will not (necessarily) succeed by making what they are used to making, like making, know how to make cheaply, or find it easy to make. The making is not or should not be the starting point. The starting point should be the wanting, the desires of customers to have something which the company will then strive to provide.

The marketing idea has certain implications. It leads to an active concern with customers, with finding out who they are, where they are, what they want, how they want it wrapped, and what they will find a convenient way to pay for it. This conception of the customer as active and determining also, and paradoxically, leads to a concern with how the customer may be influenced. So that the marketing idea is the mainspring for promotional advertising, for the psychological study of the customer, and for attempts to manipulate his desires. The marketing idea also serves to raise the status of the marketing function, largely at the expense of production, and to endow with a higher importance the things that marketing people do. This leads to the second understanding of marketing, namely, marketing as a totality, and at an operating level this is the important one.

Marketing as a totality is based on the realisation that a variety of considerations and operations are involved in getting people to buy things; it is not just a matter of selling in the strict sense. So, for example, marketing is concerned with pricing, with decisions about the range of products on offer and how to price them, with whether to have a tiered pricing system in the sense of, say, different prices for the trade and the general public. Marketing is concerned with advertising, with the medium in which advertising occurs, with the periodicity of advertising, and how much to spend on it. Marketing is concerned with doing research on the market, with finding out how big a potential market may be, with ascertaining the economic and demographic characteristics of buyers or users, with establishing what they want, what they would buy more of, pay more for, or can be talked into wanting. Marketing apprehends that there is something in between the factory which makes things and the customers who buy them, and that something is a distribution system. So marketing makes decisions about the kind of distribution system that will be effective in particular cases: does one sell to customers direct, by mail order, by having them come to the work in trucks and pick it up, by siting kiosks on street corners; or does one use stockists, or wholesalers, or deal direct with retailers, and if so, does one stick to retail chains or any retailers who are ready, willing, and able? And marketing is interested in analysing the results of sales: not just how much profit was made, but how and where it was made. Which customers, which areas, which product lines, indeed which salesmen are yielding most. At the same time marketing wants to know how the company is doing comparatively. Who else is in the market, are they bigger or smaller, what are the competitors respective market shares, is this situation changing and to whose advantage?

In short marketing is a complex and omnibus operation, involving a lot of different decisions, and one may be able to make gains by putting in effort at different stages in the process. This is marketing as a totality.

Marketing as a euphemism is quite trivial but needs to be mentioned both for the sake of completeness and to avoid confusion. This is an English rather than world phenomenon and amounts quite simply to the fact that a function, department, or individual manager may be given the label 'marketing' but in fact be no more than 'sales' simply because marketing is thought to sound nicer or more imposing. So any given marketing director may simply be organising the efforts of a fleet of salesmen and not doing all the things described above as belong to marketing as a totality.

Sales on the other hand is the main line of variable activity described in chapter 3. Sales is about finding customers and getting to them; about demonstrating, bargaining, persuading, closing deals, and taking orders.

The whole sales operation, as suggested earlier, is suffused with the search for information and understanding – about the potential customer's needs, budget, sensitive areas, and real motivation. The point is worth repeating since it tends to cut across the popular image of the salesman as dynamic persuader rather than sensitive listener, whereas it is argued here that the salesman usually needs to be both.

The distinction between sales and marketing may be blurred in practice, and not only by the phenomenon of sales-labelled-as-marketing described above. The blurring occurs in two ways. First, in a sales-only company some of these marketing activities will be discharged, albeit in a less systematic way, by the salesmen anyway. Salesmen will pass on and up ideas about customer wants, feelings about price increases, suggestions about how and where to go to tap new markets, and so on. Second, if salesmen do not do these things, general management or the managing director may, certainly in the sense of taking major decisions about, say, pricing policy, the distribution system, or advertising budgets. So the distinction between marketing and sales, while important and genuinely connoting meaningful differences, is not a cut and dried distinction.

Now to return to the theme of managers going abroad, the basic point is that the marketing in the full sense outlined above tends to be done at home; the marketing is the home-country activity or head-office decision. Managers who go abroad are typically involved in sales, or in activities directly in support of selling. On the other hand, sending salesmen or managers abroad is not the only way in which companies end up with overseas customers. At this stage it is helpful to consider the possibilities.

OVERSEAS SELLING IN CONTEXT

A common way whereby the products of a company come to be bought by nationals of another country is by that company establishing manufacturing facilities in the foreign country. This is not an original idea, everyone knows that many companies in all sorts of countries are off-shoots of companies with head offices in other countries. The point here is simply to note that this method of establishing manufacturing subsidiaries in other countries constitutes 'exports by another name'. The effect is the same, namely earnings abroad repatriated to the home country. It is the essence of the operations of American multinationals. Students are often surprised to learn that the USA has an unfavourable trade balance (imports exceed exports): it does not matter because of the volume of 'indirect exports'. Not of course that the establishment of overseas manufacturing subsidiaries is an American preserve. The Skefko, Electrolux, and Alfa Laval factories in Britain, for instance, are part of the Swedish export effort; the BP refineries and ICI works in West Germany are part of the British export effort, and so on.

A variation on the theme of overseas manufacturing is for a company to authorise manufacture under licence in a foreign country. In this case the company in country A allows a company in country B to make and sell its products in return for various licensing fees or royalties. Thus the products as designed and patented by the country A company are both manufactured and sold in country B. But again the effect is the same in the form of income earned abroad remitted to the initiating company in country A. This manufacture under licence tends to be a medium-sized solution: that is, it tends to be favoured by companies not large enough to have the resources to establish factories abroad, or by companies who estimate the size of the foreign market not big enough to justify such an investment.

There are a few cases where a company's sales to a foreign country are handled by credit houses. These credit houses will take produce from the selling company, look after insurance and shipments, and sell it in other countries. The seller gets fast payment, and the buyer usually benefits from having credit facilities arranged.

Much more common than this is the establishment of overseas sales subsidiaries. By definition they do not manufacture abroad, but engage in selling and where appropriate provide after sales service and handle customer relations. Normally these sales subsidiaries are staffed by nationals of the country in which they are located, which is cheaper than sending out managers from the base country, and may make better sense in cultural and linguistic terms as well. Sometimes, however, such sales subsidiaries are established or headed-up by expatriate managers.

Many companies, however, use agents in foreign countries. An agent is locally based, that is, resides in the foreign country in which the company seeks to sell its goods, and is usually a national of that foreign country. The agent seeks to sell the goods of the company which has engaged his services, and does so for a commission. The advantage of agents is obvious. They speak the language, literally and metaphorically, of the country in which they are operating, and put their local knowledge and contacts at the service of companies which engage them. Agents often work for a variety of foreign companies, or principals as they are known in 'agent-speak', usually offering potential customers a coherent range of complementary products rather than competing products. Agents do not usually hold stocks. They seek orders from customers, and when they get them the principal supplies the goods required.

Sometimes the agents are owners of retail outlets, but this is not invariable and depends on the type of product concerned. In some countries, especially in the Middle East and Far East, the agent is not so much a medium which the exporting company may choose, rather than the establishment of sales subsidiaries for instance, but a condition of market entry. In these countries, that is, it is made clear to the would-be exporting company that 'everyone has an agent here' and that 'in practical terms you can't do business without an agent'. Then it usually happens that the speaker has in mind someone (younger brother) who is dreadfully reliable and unbelievably well-connected who will make an ideal agent.

An alternative to the use of agents is the employment of distributors. A distributor differs from an agent by actually buying the exporting company's products and then finding customers for them but at a somewhat higher price. Unlike the agent, the distributor may well engage in local advertising; the distributor will carry stock, will usually carry spare parts, and assume responsibility for service. The pattern is that exporting companies tend to use distributors rather than agents where their products are more complicated technically, at least to the point of consisting of many parts or components and therefore needing a supply of spare parts and service. On the other hand if the product is too big or too expensive a distributor could not afford to hold stocks of it.

To give one or two practical examples a company that makes, say, biscuits is likely to use agents in foreign countries. It is not necessary to hold stocks and the items have low unit value. What is more biscuits do not need spare parts or a 5000-mile service! But a manufacturer of, say, bicycles will probably use distributors. Spare parts and service are required, and bicycles are not so expensive as to preclude the holding of stocks. When it comes to airliners, however, even though the spare parts and service argument holds, they are clearly far too expensive for anyone to hold stocks of them.

Finally, companies may engage in direct selling abroad. They may, that is, send out their salesmen to contact known or potential customers to take or win orders. With a few minor omissions this then is the spectrum of possibilities: manufacturing abroad, manufacturing under licence abroad, use of credit houses, overseas marketing subsidiaries, use of agents, use of distributors, and direct selling. In practice the distinctions are not always as neat as in the foregoing account, and various 'mixed types' occur.

First of all the same company may use different methods in different parts of the world. One possibility is that agents are used in some countries but distributors in others. Another is that direct selling by the company's own salesmen exists side by side with the use of agents, sometimes even in the same territory. These choices may simply reflect what is available in various countries, and reflect different levels of economic development. In some cases there may be no distributors and perhaps the selling company does not have the renown or stature to find or establish them. In another country perhaps the available agents will seem of such poor quality that the exporting company will go for direct selling, even where this poses logistical problems.

Often people feel that the critical distinction is between direct selling on the one hand and the use of any intermediary – agents, distributors, concessionaires, or whatever – on the other, in the conviction that direct selling is more dynamic and purposeful. At least the company's own salesmen, it is reasoned, cannot suffer from divided loyalties as can agents. In fact a distinction in these terms is probably not valid. Direct selling is relatively unusual. The two factors which tempt companies into direct selling are usually company size and market size. Small companies, that is, may have difficulty finding agents, who tend to be understandably attracted to more substantial and big-name companies. Thus direct selling may be the only option. Or again if the overseas market is a small one then direct selling becomes viable in that the company's representative can actually hope to get round all the customers in the course of a sales trip, and it is not necessary to have agents for the purpose of coverage. To give a contrasted example in Africa one would use agents in Nigeria but direct selling in Malawi. It should be added that these thoughts about the choice of different means are generalisations, not iron laws, and there will be exceptions in practice. With this picture of the various institutional arrangements for selling overseas as background we can now pose the question, what exactly do salesmen do abroad?[1]

THE SALESMAN ABROAD

Most of all salesmen or sales managers on trips abroad are visiting their agents. The purpose is to exhort, inform, liaise, and monitor progress. The exercise is analogous to the home-based sales manager visiting his salesmen in the provinces for the purposes of encouragement and control, except that the agents abroad are not employees of the company in the manner of domestic salesmen.

In the case of companies which employ agents overseas the visiting sales manager is still likely to meet customers abroad, usually with the arrangements being made by the agent. That is to say, the agent will probably decide which customers are big and influential enough to warrant a personal visit by the sales manager, or which potential customers are likely to be won over by negotiating with the sales manager personally. It is normal for the agent to set the itinery for such customer visits, accompany the visiting sales manager, socio-culturally stage-manage the visits, and where necessary act as interpreter as well.

There is sometimes a twist to the agenda for these sales manager-agent-customer meetings which should not be disguised. This is that they are on occasion intended as a blood-letting. Where customers are known to be dissatisfied with, say, the delivery performance (goods arriving late), quality standards, or service of the exporting company, the agent may well try to 'buy them off' by letting them give the direct representative of the company, the sales manager, a good tongue lashing (at least this will stop them blaming the agent for a while!). While these blood-letting sessions are not a great deal of fun for the visiting sales manager they do constitute legitimate work. A customer with grievances has to be faced, and will probably feel better for having had a top-level moan anyway. What is more it is an opportunity for the manager to offer apologies and explanations, to try to sort out practical problems, perhaps make amends in a tangible way with discounts or free spares or an extended warranty, and at least take the complainant out to lunch.

Occasionally the sales manager abroad will be choosing or vetting agents. This is not an everyday occurrence, and usually agent–principal relations are enduring. But sometimes a company will drop an agent for under-performance, because there has been some change in the agent's mix of principals which one particular company thinks will work against their interest, or even because some particular individual working for the agent who handled the business of the company concerned has left. And of course companies attempting to enter a new geographical market may need to recruit agents there for the first time.

Most of what has been said about agents applies to distributors as well. Sales managers on trips abroad, that is, will visit their distributors to praise and blame, inform and exchange, and to generally foster the relationship. Again, occasionally, the sales manager will be looking for new distributors. And as usual distributors may well arrange for the sales manager to meet leading or critical customers, critical in either sense.

Sometimes the sales manager abroad will be engaged in direct selling, in seeing customers without the help/presence of an intermediary agent or distributor. As said it is either relatively small companies which are likely to do this, or companies operating in a relatively small foreign market. Furthermore this direct selling is more likely to be repeat-order selling than new selling; the sales manager, that is, is more likely to be seeing existing customers about further business than meeting potential new customers. The latter does, however, occur but still differs from domestic selling in that there is less 'cold-calling' and much more setting up of meetings in advance of the trip. The manager will have exploited his or his company's contacts while at home to seek out likely customers, will perhaps have used his country's consular service, or some government agency dedicated to assisting manufacturers to export, such as the British Overseas Trade Board.

Two last things should be added to this litany of sales-manager activities. One is that sales managers go to trade fairs, to represent their company, man the exhibition stand, give demonstrations of products, and of course to meet both new and existing customers at the exhibition. Some of these trade fairs are so renowned that it is almost impossible for a company of standing not to be represented at them. In Western Europe the Hanover trade fair for the mechanical engineering industry, or the Frankfurt book fair for publishers, are cases in point. Attending a trade fair may be a one-off activity, or it may be part of a more sustained foreign trip encompassing various of the 'salesman abroad' activities outlined above.

The last thing concerns very big sales deals. If a very big deal is being concluded in the foreign country then it may well be closed by the top manager of the exporting company no matter how the deal was arrived at – by the initiative of local agents, expatriate salesmen, or whatever. If the size of the deal and the importance of the customer warrants it the managing director or even chairman of the board may come out to sign the contract or conclude the formalities.

These are, broadly speaking, the things that sales managers do abroad, but what are the difficulties involved in doing them?

WHAT ARE THE PROBLEMS?

In so far as sales managers abroad are engaging in direct selling then they have all the problems encountered by domestic salesmen and alluded to in chapter 3 – the scramble for sales leads, entrées, information and clues; the stress of presenting, persuading, and hoping to close deals. One must simply note that on average export salesmen do less of this than domestic salesmen.

In their more extensive contacts with agents and distributors sales managers face a somewhat different problem, namely that of maintaining the morale, energy, and commitment of people who, although they stand to benefit from the success of the company, are not its direct employees and may well have other loyalties. These people are also by definition operating 'at a distance' from the exporting company, so that control is in any case more problematic. To put it positively, the sales manager is visiting them to make sure they keep up the good work, to advise, inform, and encourage. Or to put it negatively, the sales manager is going out there to try to overcome the natural lethargy and divided loyalties of his company's agents.

A further difficulty already noted is the sales manager's occasional need to 'take stick' from dissatisfied customers. This occurs in domestic selling as well but tends to be more poignant in export sales. This is partly because there is more scope for something to go wrong if a product is being sent abroad, more chance of loss, delay, or damage, and it is logistically more difficult to put it right. What is more where this has happened the customer is more likely to have 'bottled up' the ensuing grievances which therefore find a correspondingly more turbulent release when someone from the company is actually there to moan at.

More pervasive than this is the strain of foreign trips. There are several dimensions to this strain. First, the sales manager abroad like his colleague at home experiences the strain of meeting a lot of people and trying to get these encounters right. The more these people the sales manager meets are new contacts as opposed to people he knows already or at least met on the last trip, the more demanding are these encounters in terms of social skills and nervous energy.

Second, foreign business trips are usually tiring in a simple physical way. In Third World countries there may be problems with climate, accommodation, and hygiene. There is the stress that follows from not being able to take for granted the things one takes for granted at home – that the taps will work, that there will be a call-box on the corner, that the taxi-driver won't stop in a side street and demand money with menaces. But even in the West an element of the foreign business trip is the continual need to check and find things, and set them up. One is always looking for something, a luggage depository, somewhere to hold a meeting with clients, the place where the airport bus stops, or whatever; and one is always checking appointments, and train times, and flight numbers.

Lastly in this connection there are the kinds of trap and challenge hinted at in the Seoul story at the start of the chapter which derive from broad social-cultural differences between countries. Most people agree that the Middle East, for instance, is difficult for Western travellers and impossibly difficult for women (Saudi Arabia will not admit foreign women for business purposes). Or again there are countries in which it is offensive to cross your legs when sitting or to point your foot at someone. In non-Christian countries the use of the word 'Christian' in such harmless phrases as 'What did you say your Christian name is' has to be avoided.

Not only is there the problem of bribery, what to do if exposed to it and how to respond if invited to offer a bribe, but in some countries the strict relationship between the government and the citizenry may pose problems for the foreign salesman. There may be cases, that is, where a military dictatorship, Communist regime, or even a religiously influenced government may impose rules or prescriptions that get in the way of normal business.

This awkward situation is given a further twist where the nationals one is dealing with propose to break or ignore such rules. What would you do, for instance, if your trading partners in Hungary suggest changing your US dollars for you at above the official rate; or someone with whom you have done a deal in Nicaragua says that although a curfew is in force after 8 p.m. it does not really apply to businessmen so it is all right to go out on the town; or your Libyan host invites you to a private drinks party?

BACK AT THE RANCH

It should be added that not all the difficulties which export sales managers face are actually encountered while they are abroad. Two recurrent species of aggro, documentation and payments, are dealt with from the home base. The documentation is simply more critical for consignments which are being exported since it may well have to be in a foreign language, it may have to conform to procedures stipulated by other countries, insurance has to be arranged, some provision must be made for paying import dues and VAT where relevant, and in some cases export licences are required. The export licence requirement usually reflects the desire of some national governments to limit the exportation of certain technologies with a military application. The problem of documentation, however, is part of the larger issue of government policy and regulations generally.

In an attempt to safeguard the products of the home country a government may introduce legislation to benefit and protect local manufacturers. In Finland, for example, the government has introduced legislation obliging all imported tractors to incorporate certain technical features including a low sound rating. The measure is meant to protect the national tractor manufacturer Valmat Tractors, and obliges foreign firms that wish to export tractors to Finland to undertake modifications to their standard models with consequent disruption of normal production runs.

Again some governments give subsidies to national producers whether the latter are exporting or simply supplying the home market: where a local foreign firm is supplying that home market it is correspondingly more difficult for others to export to that country because their products are less likely to be competitive in price. Japan, India, and the Iron Curtain countries offer such subsidies and are in that measure putting up barriers to would-be exporters to these countries.

In some countries governments which are worried about the trade balance or the dissipation of their foreign currency reserves may impose import quotas. In such cases, Trinidad is one example, it becomes necessary to obtain import licences, and even where these are granted they may be for a reduced quota of goods. So, for instance, a company 'wins' an export order for, say, $25 000 worth of goods but when the import licence comes through the amount has changed to $18 000. In Kenya, to give another example, these quotas are fixed in the light of the value of the previous year's exports to that country by any foreign company. This means that the value of imports is held down and in fact reduced in real value by inflation.

Indeed the list of such obstacles is endless. In Japan there are stringent regulations about the ingredients which go into biscuits, involving biscuit exporters to that country in recipe changes and production difficulties. In New Zealand there are duties of up to 50% on computer parts to encourage the development of the domestic electronics industry. In the Iron Curtain countries there is a general reluctance to part with hard (Western) currency for anything, and pressure is put on Western exporters to these countries to engage in counterpart trade, that is, to accept payment in kind.

Politics as well as policies play a part in international trade. To start with a zaney example the explosion of crude oil prices in 1973 led to a more equitable distribution of wealth in some of the Middle East countries: this, however, has worked against exporters of high-quality, expensive, luxury items to these areas! Countries with centrally planned economies, Russia being the example *par excellence*, often cause difficulties in international trade because of their spasmodic and unpredictable demand patterns. To burlesque it a little, one year there will be some concession to consumerism and the import of jeans and video toys will be allowed, the next year these quotas will be blocked entirely and it will be machine tools or nothing.

Some countries do not like other countries. The former French colonies rarely buy anything from Britain, for example. It is part of the French genius to have culturally annexed its colonies (and besides that they get a 10–15% price preference when they deal with France). Libya does not like doing business with Britain, but is relaxing a bit because they dislike the USA even more. The Far East countries are not anti-British, but are pro-American, because of the American aid that poured in after the Second World War and on account of the number of nationals from these countries who have been to college in the USA. Sweden is adept at exploiting its pacifist, neutralist, and socialist stance in trade dealings with both the Communist countries and the Third World.

Arranging payment is another problem for exporting countries, since transactions are often paid for not in cash but by opening what are called 'letters of credit'. Now, firstly, there may be a problem about whether the letter of credit is irrevocable (does not permit the buyer to change his mind!), and secondly there may be difficulty in the timing of the letter of credit. It may be the case that the letter of credit is not received at the time the export order is secured, but months afterwards. Or again, the letter of credit never materialises and the would-be exporter has to dispose of a partly or wholly manufactured consignment in some other way.

In Africa much business is done in the form of aid relief, in turn arranged by a Central Tender Board financed by the World Bank. The exporting company is not paid until the funds come through from the World Bank and this may take a year. Not only the Warsaw Pact countries but also Chile and Brazil do not want money leaving the country, so that companies which export to these areas, as suggested earlier, are asked to take goods in return. This in its turn tends to favour exporters who are not only large but conglomerate (made up of lots of different product-businesses with no logical connection between them). So that if, for instance, a British civil engineering company builds a harbour in Poland and a motorway in Brazil it is easier to accept payment in screws and coffee respectively if the civil engineering firm is part of a conglomerate sporting mechanical engineering firms and a supermarket chain!

Finally in this connection a company's products may simply be unsuitable for export, even without any artificial constraint of the Finnish tractor legislation kind. Many textile manufacturers, for example, cannot export their shirts to Sweden because the Swedes like to wear only all-cotton shirts. Or our favourite example, biscuits are a case in point. British biscuits are undoubtedly the best in the world. But other countries are not equal in their capacity to enjoy the benefits conferred by the British biscuit manufacturer, in that the export of chocolate and cream biscuits to non-temperate climes is hardly viable. This picturesque point opens up a related issue, namely that of the relationship between the export sales department and the production function.

In short this relationship is variable. In companies with a long record of exporting, and especially in companies where a high proportion of all produce is exported, the export sales–production relationship will tend to be satisfactory. At least there will be a general acceptance that exports matter and overseas customers have to be treated with respect. On the other hand there are companies where the volume or proportion of exports does not amount to much, where the prevalent attitude concerning exports is that it is a lot of hassle over forms and payment systems and for what, for a smaller mark-up than one can get at home. And where export orders need some modification or special treatment in production, as in noiseless tractors for Finland, then resentment or irritation may be generated. The tractor example is by no means an isolated case. There are plenty of products where at least by convention different sizes are required in other countries. Imagine being a British carpet manufacturer, and every twelfth carpet has to be of a different width because it is going to continental Europe.

HOME AND ABROAD: IS THERE A DIFFERENCE?

To round off this discussion of export selling it is worth asking if the work of domestic and export salesmen or sales managers differs systematically. Clearly the two jobs have much in common. They are centred in sales rather than marketing, they involve direct interface with actual or potential customers, and call for the same blend of sensitive listening and persuasive talking. On the other hand there are some differences.

The most obvious one is that when the export manager is at home rather than abroad, and home is where they spend most of their time, they are engaged not so much on sales but on sales administration. That is, they have more office work, more paperwork. The export salesman at home is responding to letters, telexes, and phone calls from agents and customers abroad. A fair amount of time may be spent in preparing quotations, specifying how much a particular product or consignment will cost an overseas customer. The quotations are more complicated than for domestic buyers because of such things as freight charges, insurance, import dues, greater cost of honouring warranties, and administration of payment systems (a euphemism for waiting for your money). Then again there will be a volume of correspondence with agents and distributors, not necessarily relating to specific orders. There is also the preparation of accompanying documents, and handling applications for import and export licences. Furthermore in some cases, as suggested in the last section, accepting export orders implies specific liaison with the production function with regard to lead times and specifications. Foreign trips also require some preparation, not just in the sense of flight bookings and hotel reservations, but preparing the substance of meetings too – going through correspondence files for particular customers, checking quotations and supporting documentation for critical sales meetings, reviewing sales performance data for agents or distributors one plans to visit, and so on. In short export sales in comparison with home sales means less direct contact with customers but more administration.

It is probably this same difference which is reflected in another, namely different modes of remuneration. In the case of domestic salesmen the amount received is typically made up of a base salary plus commission. In some cases, indeed, there are different levels of commission for the same individual, whereby reaching a certain level of commission earnings in a given time period in itself warrants a bonus. Understandably, strongly commission-based remuneration packages are most common for domestic salesmen who are involved in the sale of high-value products to first-time buyers – computer salesmen are a good example. Export salesmen or sales managers, however, tend to be on a straight salary.

This in turn reflects the indirect nature of much export selling, where often the actual seeking out and winning over of new customers is not done by the sales manager but by agents on the spot. Where this indirect system operates it is not such an obviously good idea to base remuneration in part on commission.

Finally, in supervising two undergraduate studies of the work of salesmen I have fallen on two other facts, at least one of which fits into the pattern. The first of these studies is an interview-based account of the work of domestic salesmen, which shows among other things that most of them have university degrees and that they change jobs quite often or expect to.[2] The second is a comparable study of export sales managers and shows among other things that most of them are not graduates and that they have fairly stable careers and career expectations.[3] The typical manager interviewed in this second study, that is, has been in his or her present company for some time, been in exporting for some time, and does not expect any dramatic change.

These two studies are based on quite small samples of British managers so too much should not be made of this contrast. Having said this the first finding, fewer graduates in export sales, is intriguing precisely because it cuts across popular expectation. After all, one would think, export selling must be at least as difficult and probably more so with a putative need for foreign languages. On the other hand the relative job stability of export managers is consistent with the nature of the work, which is specialised in a peculiar way. It is not, that is, a technical specialism, but an experiential one. It depends very much on knowing a set of people, cultures, and routines. As such these export jobs are not easy to drop in and out of, there is a premium on cashing in on the hard-won experience of the past. After all it takes a certain maturity to keep a clear head in the private suite of a hotel in downtown Seoul.

NOTES

1 An excellent background book to the foreign sales operation discussed in this chapter is: Peter Turnbull and Malcolm Cunningham (1981) *International Marketing and Purchasing*, Macmillan, London. It describes the strengths and weaknesses of half a dozen European countries, including Britain, in the area of buying and selling to other countries.

2 This study of the work of domestic salesmen is: John Mansfield, No Prizes for Coming Second, unpublished undergraduate dissertation, Department of Management Studies, University of Loughborough, 1983.

3 The corresponding study of the work of export sales managers is: Joanna Dunn, Insight into Export Selling, unpublished undergraduate dissertation, Department of Management Studies, University of Loughborough, 1985.

7

Challenge and Culture

The previous chapter looked at export sales both as a business operation of some complexity and as the activity which most frequently takes managers abroad. The present chapter is in a sense a sequel focusing on the increasing number of managers who experience foreign placements as opposed to making business trips aboad. Experiencing a difference of culture is a *leitmotiv* in this discussion of what happens to managers who are sent to work abroad by their companies, and the chapter ends by examining a recent attempt to formulate at least work-related cultural differences in a systematic way.

HAVE SKILLS, WILL TRAVEL

Perhaps the most surprising thing about the expatriate manager phenomenon is the range of missions on which managers are sent overseas. Certainly sales and product-development assignments account for a share of these overseas postings but there are many other reasons besides. In classifying these missions one can make a broad distinction between ongoing positions and project work. Ongoing position assignments are where a manager is sent out to be in charge of someting which is already 'up and running' – a sales office, an overseas manufacturing subsidiary, a joint venture – and when this manager's tour is finished he will normally be replaced by someone else. Project assignments, on the other hand, tend to be exploratory, innovative, or one-off. The project is taken to completion (or occasionally abandoned as non-viable) and that is it, mission accomplished. To get some feel for the variety of assignments which managers may have abroad, consider a dozen or so examples, some from my range of manager acquaintances but most from a recent study of expatriate British managers:[1]

— to run a sales office in Japan for 3 years
— to run a manufacturing subsidiary in South Africa
— to set up from scratch and then stay on to run a marketing subsidiary in Brazil
— to go to Copenhagen and take over a Sales HQ for Scandinavia, setting targets and budgets for the national sales office in each of the Scandinavian countries, monitoring performance and appointing key staff as needed
— to do a feasibility study in Austria, to decide if it is worth setting up a factory there to supply Austria and southern Germany.
— to develop new raw materials and suppliers thereof in several countries in the Far East; that is, to locate sources of supply and instruct potential suppliers in how to process the raw materials to meet the needs of the company in Britain.
— the company has recently bought its former agents (see previous chapter) in France, and the mission is to up-grade this agency to the status of a proper marketing subsidiary, recruiting the necessary additional staff in France
— the company concerned has recently acquired a factory in Italy, but just after the acquisition the personnel manager leaves; the expatriate managers's mission is to fill the gap, establish standardised personnel systems at the Italian factory, and to recruit and train a successor.
— to help the British-owned company in the USA manufacture for the first time the biggest and dearest product in the range which hitherto has only been made in Britain; it involves identifying and organising a ring of component suppliers in the USA to make the operation independent
— to sort out a recently acquired factory in France that is, to

show them how to plan the volume of production to integrate with the needs of the British owner and to institute quality control (inspection) procedures compatible with those in the rest of the group

— to act as technical liaison officer between a British company and its Nigerian business partner company selling and maintaining British equipment in West Africa; shortly after arrival in Nigeria the head of the company resigned so the English expatriate manager ran the whole company for 3 years

And a last example combining the colourful and the complex:

— to go to Houston for 2 years to assist an American multinational pet-food manufacturer to exploit a possible new, high-protein pet food ingredient source, namely small fish; it is really a threefold mission: to find out where these fish are world-wide and in what numbers; to figure a way to get them into the cans fast (so that pet owners are not put off by an unduly fishy smell!); to convince senior managers in the group that savings can be made by using some fish in recipes that are normally all animal based.

Before looking at some of the things involved in carrying out these assignments, it is worth considering the impact of such foreign placements on the families concerned. Or to put it more jauntily, take up what one writer has described as 'the knotty problem of the wife'.[2]

THE BIG DECISION

In a generally complicated world there is at any rate one simple choice. The wives of managers who are sent abroad by their companies either go with them or stay at home. In the study cited above[3] the majority in fact stayed at home, though it has to be said that this is only a small sample. Typical reasons for staying at home, even where the husband is going to be abroad for 2 or 3 years, are having a job (and a part-time job may be a sufficient anchor to the home country), not wanting to disrupt children's schooling, and more often a reluctance to take very little children abroad.

All the managers interviewed after the event claimed that their wives had coped very well on their own, though this does not necessarily mean the husbands had not been worrying about them on this account. Some of the husbands confess to quite enjoying the freedom of being on their own at first, but missing their families and loneliness take over, with partings after return visits being especially poignant. As one interviewed manager recalled: 'I remember one time sitting in the first-class section of a jumbo jet, flying off overseas, eating caviar and sipping iced vodka. I sat there and felt really lonely and fed up and remember realising the irony of the whole situation.'[4]

On the other hand keeping the family together is not always an unmitigated success. The corresponding problem is the possibility of acute boredom for the wife, cut off from her normal circle of friends but without the husband's contacts at work. If house boys, gardeners, and servants are provided, and this is common on placements in the Third World, then there is not very much to do, and it is often difficult or downright impossible for the wife of an expatriate manager to get a job abroad. The worst is where an unemployed wife, surrounded by servants in a country whose language she does not speak, is left on her own for 10 days while her husband flies home to discuss his corporate plan at head office. There is, however, one standard refuge for both lonely husbands and bored wives – the expatriate community – of which more later.

CULTURE IN ACTION

Culture may be a vague word but looking at the experiences of expatriate managers gives it a more tangible form. First of all many of them are confronted with a foreign language. They usually make an attempt to learn it, and their companies often send them on mind-erodingly intensive language courses before they leave, but it takes a long time really to master a new language. In the early stages one is also torn two ways. It is always possible to make some headway in English, to seek to work through those local managers who do speak it well, and hang the rest. This gets things done, and saves the expatriate having to make a fool of himself by speaking a foreign language badly. In the short term this seems the ideal solution, and fluency will no doubt come. The trouble is that the short term all too easily becomes the long term and 2 years later the expatriate is still surrounded by those English speakers he feels comfortable with. The man of character will, as they say in school-teaching circles, 'start the way he means to go on', in broken Rumanian or whatever, but it takes some resolution to do this.

There is a variation on the language theme. Sometimes it does not matter much whether or not the expatriate learns the foreign language, either because he is part of an expatriate task force and all his contacts are with fellow countrymen, or because all the local managers do speak English, on account of the dominance of English as a business language. Managers in this situation can get by easily as far as work in the narrow sense is concerned, but find themselves cut off from more sustained social and leisure contacts with local managers or local people generally. Little incidents sharply remind them they are in a foreign culture, when for instance local managers exchange asides in German or revert to Danish at lunch.

As can be seen from the examples of expatriate manager assignments these tend to cast the expatriate in the role of leader, innovator, animator. When this fact is combined with the culture gap it is not surprising that expatriates on occasion meet with scepticism and mistrust on the part of the locals, and this reaction is by no means restricted to Third World countries. Indeed expatriate managers sometimes speak of a 'white doctor' phenomenon, of the need to produce at an early stage some miraculous cure to convince the locals that they really do know how to set up a production control system or a marketing subsidiary.

One of the classics of nineteenth-century sociology depicts the emergence of modern society in terms of the transition from *Gemeinschaft* to *Gesellschaft*, from community to association.[5] In this formulation *Gemeinschaft* is rural, primary, emotive, and oriented to the extended family and its claims, whereas *Gesellschaft* is urban, secondary, rational, and oriented to contractual relationships with occupants of particular roles and statuses. The point of this brief excursion into sociological theory is to say that much of the world is (still) more *Gemeinschaft* than *Gesellschaft*, and this fact comes up in the testimonies of expatriate managers in Third World countries. A common theme here is that locals have difficulty in accepting the expatriate simply as a role incumbent, as a professional manager sent out by the owning company because he 'knows his stuff'. Local managers, in other words, feel a need to know the expatriate as a person before doing business with him as a role incumbent. But if you are the expatriate, you need to know this, and it all takes time.

Another dimension of the culture gap is the possibility of being exposed to something abroad that is unknown at home. To give an obvious example, contrasts of wealth and poverty are much sharper in the Third World. Imagine living in an executive bungalow in a leafy suburb of Rio de Janeiro and from your patio you can see the bidonville lower down the hill where people are living in cardboard boxes. Or to work in Nigeria where it is too dangerous to drive on out of town roads at night, and in the day-time urban traffic jams make it literally quicker to walk. Imagine having to pay a bribe to see a dentist, get the post delivered, or renew your library book.

There are of course more subtle variations on this theme, and one does not have to go a long way from home to find them. One expatriate manager observed in the course of an interview that 'life experiences and the company put together had not prepared me for the differences in temperament between the French and the English'.[6] In other words, logic patterns were different, attitudes and conventions contrasting. Another manager interviewed was struck by the unevenness of Italian friendliness: 'Italians are very friendly in general but when it comes to their own home, they see this as a very personal environment and do not draw outsiders into this easily or quickly.'[7] Or again, an expatriate family in Japan found they made many acquaintances but no real friends.

Within a 3-year period they were invited into just two Japanese homes. Language difficulties obviously contributed towards the barriers present but the main factor was the distinction between the Western and Eastern culture: 'Westerners don't know the niceties and ways of establishing yourself in Japan', and 'The Japanese have little contact with Westerners and therefore don't know how to relate to them'. The couple found it difficult to know how to try to fit in.

THE EXPAT COMMUNITY AND THE FUN CULTURE

The importance of cultural differences is paradoxically underlined by the existence in many countries, and especially in their capital cities, of expatriate communities with common sets of activities and a fairly pronounced 'fun culture'. Where these expatriate communities exist they exert a strong pull on managers abroad, with or without their families, and provide a kind of cocoon location in which all leisure may be spent.

What makes an expatriate community? Well firstly of course sizable numbers of expatriates, enough for common activities and club membership. But secondly the *sine quo non* is that they should be foreigners in the location being considered; they do not have to be groups of English or Americans abroad. Expatriate communities in capital cities indeed tend to be heterogeneous in the sense of the national origins of their members, but homogeneous in other ways. To start with they tend to be drawn from high-income, high-status occupations – the business community, diplomacy, management, employment in international organisations, business schools, or international universities. So they tend to be cosmopolitan in outlook, they are all foreigners in the country concerned and they develop a 'highest common denominator' expatriate culture. At the level of common activities expensive sports and group hedonism predominate: dinner parties, cocktail parties, barbecues, beach parties, skiing, scuba diving, and so on. The whole thing is 'hyped' with a 'we're all in the same boat' and 'let's have fun abroad' disposition, and easy camaraderie blooms. Insular Americans who would think twice before crossing the Mississippi–Alabama state line think nothing of partnering Malawians at bridge or tennis at the expat club; Londoners who have never crossed the North Circular Road (unless by air) accept Norwegians and even Glaswegians as equals.

But the interesting thing is that the expatriate community is the product of push as well as pull. Expatriates, that is, are not only drawn to these communities by thoughts of uncomplicated fellowship and iced bacardi, they feel themselves propelled towards them as well by the complexities of local culture. So that the expat community is a cultural refuge: it saves you having to learn Danish or whatever (expat communities all have English as lingua franca), it releases one from the burden of learning about and adapting to the national culture of the country concerned, and expat communities are quite incomparable as safety valves. They offer the chance to get together with other non-nationals and denounce the place you are in, tell psycho-release stories about the dreadful blunders one made in the first week of the posting, and endlessly to anecdotalise the 'quaint little ways' of the locals. In other words the popularity of expatriate communities is a stark testimony to the challenging difference between national cultures.

OH TO BE IN ENGLAND

When managers accept initiatives from their companies to send them abroad they tend to think they will do well out of it in the short term, and they are right. Those who think about their eventual return to the home country also tend to assume that they will do well, that they will make some career capital out of the foreign posting so long as they have not 'fouled up'. This assumption tends to be right as well, but in a less immediate and less tangible way than those involved expect. Or to put it more broadly, there are some 're-entry' problems when expatriate managers return to their home country.

Those who have been abroad on their own often have readjustment problems with their own families, no matter how much they have missed them. At a quite simple level they are used to not-sharing accommodation (no arguments about the toothpaste and no children's toys under their feet). Returning families, on the other hand, are usually confronted with a lower standard of living, because of all the perks associated with a foreign posting, which tend to induce a kind of 'duty-free' living. The fact that little children have short memories also comes into play in this connecton when they disarmingly claim not to be able to remember their home country.

Returning managers also often have a sense of being 'personally reduced' on their return. Abroad they were top dogs, running the show, representing the company, the voice of New York City in the Venezuelan outback. But at home they are just 'some guy who has been abroad for a couple of years and doesn't know the latest around here'. This last bit is especially significant: not only does the returning expat not know what has been going on in his national company, but he has not been able to take advantage of the usual flux of change and opportunity. Hence it is not unusual for returning managers to speak of having 'missed out' in terms of career development. Politically important relationships they might have built up within the company have lapsed, alliances have gone cold, work assignments have been reorganised without one having been present to take advantage of the change, promotion vacancies have come and gone, and so forth. All this might be countered by instant promotion, but instant promotion is not generally forthcoming.

The plus side, however, is substantial. Expatriate managers often return with new language skills in the narrow sense and enhanced communication skills in a larger sense. They have a feeling of having been prime movers abroad, of having made things happen, of doing things beyond the managerial routine, of demanding assignments carried through. All this is very good for personal self-confidence. It is also good for exposure in the company. The expatriate is marked out by his experience and achievement. He has done something that most of this colleagues have not done, and the presumption is he can do difficult and demanding things again.

MANAGEMENT AND THE WIDER WORLD

There is a sense in which the testimony of this chapter and the last one is at odds with what has gone before. In examining both the work of export salesmen and the experiences of expatriate managers, differences in national cultures have been highlighted. Yet the rest of the account, and indeed most accounts of management, treat management as a universal, as something which is the same everywhere. Is it?

Until about 10 years ago most authorities would have said that it was. This former general conviction as to the homogeneity of management had as its starting point a concept of industrialisation as a world force cutting across national boundaries, imposing its own demands and shaping its own uniformities. Although countries differ in the degree to which they are industrialised, differ in when industrialisation did (or might) begin, and even in the speed with which industrialisation was (will be) accomplished, the assumption is that industrialisation as a process is the same.[8]

In other words, industrialisation is seen as consisting of the same elements: replacing human muscle power with machines, concentrating people in places of work (factories!), breaking down complex tasks into manageable segments and re-combining the output (division of labour), vastly raising the scale of production and practising 'economies of scale' in its administration. So far so good, but less tangible and more speculative elements became 'welded on' to this basic idea of industrialisation as a set of tangible measures for the organising of increased output.

The first of these is that it is rational. That those who initiated industrialisation, capitalist entrepreneurs, were motivated by a desire for personal wealth and would therefore go about the operation in a rational and orderly way. Second, a notion of transferable efficiency was generated. Clearly industry involves employing resources – materials, people, equipment – to generate an output – goods or services. But the amount of the output is variable, so that the ratio of resources to output is a measure of efficiency. This formulation is popularly used in statements of the, for instance, how many man hours it takes to make a motor car, how much it costs to put a student through medical school, how many kilowatts of electricity are consumed in smelting a given amount of aluminium, kind. Now the idea of transferable efficiency is an important prop to the assumption that industrialisation is homogeneous. It must be, goes the implicit argument, because all will seek to measure efficiency and to adopt the 'one best way' to get it right – and this will be the same in Tokyo as it is in Topeka, Kansas.

A third assumption concerns management. Industrialisation's generic units, companies, need these people called managers to run them. But because, as we have agreed, industrialisation is a rational, orderly process, striving for universal efficiency, with standardising effect, these managers will clearly be the same sort of people doing the same things in the same ways – and if any diverge, laws of profit, efficiency and rationality will pull them back on course. The last assumption concerns the companies themselves. The view is that manufacturing companies, these generic units of industrialisation, will be much the same with regard to their structure and general features wherever they are located. At any rate, it used to be assumed that this would be true for countries at the same stage of industrial development having the same sort of political system; say, for instance, advanced industrial societies which are also parliamentary democracies. Thus, for example, one would not expect any difference in, say, automobile firms whether located in Dagenham or Detroit City, Turin or Cologne. This is a short version of the case for the prosecution, the case assuming or alleging that industry, management and manufacturing companies are everywhere and always the same. The case is no longer accepted, at least not without hefty qualifications. The last few years have seen a renewed general interest in national differences, and this interest has been focused particularly on phenomena relating to national economic performance. Thus we have had comparative studies of the extent of company divisionalisation, comparisons of company structure, of the operation of industrial apprenticeship schemes, of systems of technical education, and of work-related attitudes. What is more this 'rediscovery of national man' movement has been buttressed by various one-off studies as well, describing, celebrating, or advocating the practices and virtues of particular countries. The valorisation of Japan in the late 1980s is the most obvious example, but Japan has had its predecessors as exemplar of economic performance.

Both to give the sense of this reserach literature and to give some more systematic form to the various references to cultural differences in this and the previous chapter, we will take two of these comparative studies. One is a modest but insightful comparison between two European countries, the second a wide-ranging overview study based on survey evidence in more than 50 countries.

THE RHINE AND THE RHONE

At a research institute in Aix-en-Provence in southern France a group of researchers have made some systematic comparisons between companies in France and West Germany. The first study concerned salary, and both coined and popularised the notion of a 'salary hierarchy'. The salary hierarchy is the spread of salaries in any one organisation, the gap, that is, between the lowest- and highest-paid persons. In a small sample of matched companies in France and West Germany it emerged that the salary hierarchy is much longer in France. Again note that this does not mean that the French, whether workers or managers, are better paid than the Germans; it means that the gap between the wage of the most poorly paid unskilled worker on the one hand and the salary of the highest paid manager on the other, is bigger in France.

It is an interesting finding. No one knew it before, and there is no obvious common-sense explanation. Also all the sub-propositions that one might infer from the global statement that the salary hierarchy is longer in France are shown to be true by this study. So, for example, the salary gap between junior and senior managers, between manual and non-manual workers, between skilled and unskilled workers, between workers and supervisors, between clerical workers and junior managers, are all bigger in the French companies in the sample.

The finding can be interpreted in several ways. One might argue that the French are more status conscious than the Germans and thus differentiate more sharply by pay the different statuses in their companies. Or it may be that the French are rewarding by higher pay a wider spread of educational qualifications than is usual in Germany. Or it may have something to do with the relative weakness of blue-collar trade unions in France, combined with the relatively high degree of unionisation among managers. But the thing to underline is that all these possible explanations deal in socio-cultural factors. In other words a 'simple study' of salary differences shows companies to be very much embedded in their national cultures, affected by traditions and values, as well as the education and industrial relations systems in those societies.

The second of these Aix-en-Provence studies is even more fascinating, and proceeds in terms of comparisons between matched samples of firms in France and West Germany. A matched sample is where the unit companies from the two countries are in contrasted pairs with technology and product held constant. Thus there is a machine-tool company in France paired with a machine-tool company in Germany, a steel firm in France and a steel firm in Germany, and so on. The idea is that by controlling these factors of product and type of industry any differences that emerge from the study can be rightly attributed to the Frenchness or Germanness of the firms. But are there any?

Just to get the flavour of the study, consider these ten findings:

— the organisational hierarchy is longer in France; there are more ranks between the ordinary worker and the chief executive/managing director.
— in most of the firms the proportion of non-manual workers is higher in the French case

— the German firms attached more importance to the *skills* of junior management and office staff
— in the German firms there was less compartmentalisation between: unskilled manual workers, skilled manual workers, technicians and non-manual workers; in the French firms each of these constitutes more of a separate group and a separate ladder of promotion
— similarly in the German firms there is less compartmentalisation between: office staff, junior management, senior management; and in the German firms there is a higher proportion of senior managers who began work as junior employees or manual workers
— in the French firms there are more supervisory personnel, and their grades are more clearly defined than in the German firms
— technical staff engaged on preparing, planning, processing, and checking work are more numerous in the French firms, but in contrast to Germany are paid less than the foreman
— the non-production personnel, that is the commercial and administrative divisions, constitute a higher proportion of the total labour force in the French firms
— these administrative and commercial personnel, and their work, enjoy higher status in France
— the German firms have more women in non-manual jobs than the French firms.

THE NATURE OF THE CONTRAST

Just consider the sharpness of the contrast between the French and German companies that can be inferred from this terse presentation of findings. With just a bit of reading between the lines and a touch of burlesque the French firms emerge as more bureaucratic. With their spread-out salary hierarchy and long chain of command they are rewarding formal authority, seniority, loyalty to the firm, and the possession of very high formal educational qualifications by management. Both vertical and horizontal distinctions among the labour force are emphasised. The proportion of indirect labour (non-production workers) is higher, and certain 'indirect' functions (administrative and commercial) carry higher status.

The German firms, on the other hand, are less graded and have a more egalitarian wage structure. There are more manual workers, more production workers, and more women in non-manual jobs; there is less emphasis on the distinction between grades and less importance is attached to seniority. There is more emphasis on the possession of skills, and the workers and foreman enjoy a higher level of technical skills/training than their French counterparts.

That is a lot of difference. What is more, the two countries concerned are not at opposite ends of the earth. They are both advanced industrial countries in Western Europe, geographically adjacent, both members of OECD, and founder members of the EEC.

CULTURE'S CONSEQUENCES

The second comparative study is the work of a Dutch psychologist, Geert Hofstede, in an impressive book with the same title as this heading.[9]

To begin with Hofstede offers a working definition of culture as collective mental programming. So that the import of national culture is a propensity on the part of citizens of particular countries to believe certain things, think in certain ways, and to engage in behaviours consistent with these thoughts and beliefs. The national 'mental programme' which may be revealed by study is an average of the citizens' convictions and behaviours, there is nothing absolute about it (not all the Swiss, for instance, want the introduction of the death penalty for parking offences, it is just a majority view!).

Hofstede's evidence derives from his work as a psychologist for an American multinational company with operations in more than 50 counties. In this capacity he administered questionnaire tests of attitudes and values to employees at a variety of levels in the many countries concerned, and for 40 of these countries the breadth and reliability of the data is sufficient for systematic analysis. Later supplementary data became available for another 10 countries, and for three multi-country regions.

It is postulated that there are four major dimensions in terms of which national cultures may be classified. It is clear that these are basic dimensions because all possible combinations exist in practice. The first of these is individualism versus collectivism, which is very much the idea of *Gemeinschaft* versus *Gesellschaft* cited a few pages earlier in discussing the experiences of expatriate managers in the Third World. In an individualist national culture a person concentrates on looking after his or herself and perhaps on their close family. In a collectivist culture, however, one has broader and more diffuse commitments to the extended family or wider group, community, or even tribe.

The most individualist country in Hofstede's survey is, wait for it, Australia, with Britain and the United States just behind, followed by Canada and the Netherlands. All the strongly collectivist national cultures are in the Third World, though with Portugal, Greece, and Yugoslavia being closer to the Third World than to Western Europe on this dimension. A further point of interest is that Hofstede correlates the country scores on the individualist–collectivist dimension with national wealth measured by GNP per capita, and there is a fairly clear patterning along the lines of the richer the country the more individualist the national culture. The two countries which deviate most from this association are Britain and Sweden, where Britain is too poor by the standards of its individualism, and Sweden is too collectivist for its wealth!

The second dimension is power distance, or the degree of tolerance for differences in power, in given national cultures. In the context of formal organisations high-power distance or a high tolerance for differences in power means in practice acceptance of autocratic leaders and high levels of centralisation. Hofstede crosses the first and second dimensions and there is quite strong patterning. The Third World countries, that is, are marked by high tolerance for differences in power together with collectivism, while most of the Western countries show up as both individualistic and low on power distance. The patterning, however, is not complete, with Belgium, France, Spain, Italy, and South Africa being relatively high on both power distance and individualism. But perhaps the most spectacularly deviant country is tiny Costa Rica which combines a high score for collectivism (like the other Third World countries) with a low tolerance of power differences. This should be seen as a further tribute to the only Latin American country that does not have a standing army!

The third dimension is uncertainty avoidance. This derives from the fact that the future is by definition unknowable, which necessarily engenders some uncertainty, even anxiety. Societies respond to this in different ways, some by cultivating a relaxed 'take life as it comes' stance, while others strive to control the future with a miscellany of planning, procedures, and contingency arrangements. On this dimension the countries do not divide at all well in relation to national wealth or economic development. The two countries with the weakest uncertainty avoidance are Singapore and Jamaica, while the next two are Denmark and Sweden. At the opposite end of the scale the two countries with the strongest uncertainty avoidance are Greece and Portugal. When the uncertainty avoidance and power distance scores are crossed there is some loose patterning with more of the Third World countries having a high tolerance for power difference and a strong uncertainty avoidance, and most of the Western countries having the reverse profile of low tolerance for power differences and weak uncertainty avoidance. The interestingly deviant group, lower on tolerance for power differences, but relatively high on uncertainty avoidance or the wish to control the future, are Germany, Austria, Switzerland, Finland, and, understandably, Israel. This last finding opens up the idea that national political experience may importantly condition the tolerance for uncertainty or need to control the future in that all these five countries, except Switzerland, are militarily, diplomatically, or politically vulnerable, or have experienced these uncertainties in the wake of the Second World War.

The fourth dimension Hofstede calls masculinity–

femininity. The starting point is that the only real difference between men and women is that men cannot have babies; all other 'differences' are socio-culturally ascribed, and vary a lot from society to society. The countries which Hofstede designates as 'masculine' are ones which maximise these sex-role differences, and ones in which 'tough' values predominate – performance, achievement, making money, showing off, glorifying power and success, and so on. The ones designated as 'feminine' are those where the dominant values, for both men and women, are those traditionally associated with the female caring role – putting relationships first, care for the small or weak, concern with the quality of life, protection of the environment, and a predisposition to the 'small is beautiful' view.

In the light of Hofstede's questionnaire data by far and away the most masculine country is Japan. Venezuela and Mexico are high on masculinity and the German-speaking group of Germany, Austria, and Switzerland are in the top half for masculinity. At the other extreme Sweden is the most feminine country, indeed the four Nordic countries plus the Netherlands constitute a little group having femininity and weak uncertainty avoidance in common. The only Third World country to achieve a femininity rating which ranks with the Nordic–Netherlands bloc is again valiant Costa Rica. Britain and the United States are in the top half for masculinity, but come lower than the German countries.

It has seemed worth spending some time on this study for several reasons. Hofstede is one of the few writers to square up to the analysis of national culture in a systematic way, and to plot the analysis in terms of four meaningful dimensions. He has also benefited from the availability of quite pricelessly extensive data.

But there is a further message. The study shows national culture differences in terms of work-related attitudes and values. The respondents have in common being employees of an American multinational company, but their values are diverse. This has implications for motivation, performance, and incentives, and even for industrial democracy, especially in a world where much of the theorising on these topics is of

American or at least Anglo-Saxon origin. It also suggests that management style is not an absolute but something which will vary from country to country. Or, in the language of the next chapter, management style is 'contextually specific'.

NOTES

1 This study of expatriate managers appears in Karen McMahon, The Foreign Experience: Expatriates Abroad, unpublished undergraduate dissertation, Department of Management Studies, University of Loughborough, 1985.

2 'The knotty problem of the wife' comes from Claire Raffael (1982), How to pick expatriates, *Management Today*, April.

3 Karen McMahon, op. cit.

4 Karen McMahon, op. cit.

5 Ferdinand Tönnies (1955) *Gemeinschaft und Gesellschaft* (*Community and Association*) translated by C. S. Loomis, Routledge & Kegan Paul, London.

6 Karen McMahon, op. cit.

7 Karen McMahon, op. cit.

8 Clark Kerr *et al.* (1960) *Industrialism and Industrial Man*, Harvard University Press, Cambridge, Mass.

9 Geert Hofstede (1980) *Culture's Consequences*, Sage Publications, Beverley Hills/London. For a neat summary see Geert Hofstede (1983) The cultural relativity of organisational practices and theories, *Journal of International Business Studies*, Fall.

8

Style and Success

There is a short story by Graham Greene in which the hero's father is killed by a pig. At the time this happened the hero was a prep-school boy and the father a minor travel writer on assignment in Italy. The father was walking with professional intent through the poorer part of Naples when an over-fed pig caused the collapse of the fifth-floor balcony on which it was tethered and plummeted into the street below with fatal effect. It should be added that this was not a remarkable event in Naples in the 1920s where the pig was as common on the balcony as the rubber plant in the modern office.

The hero of Greene's short story suffered a double blow. He lost a father of whom he was very fond, and was lumbered with an embarrassing story. The second affliction grew worse with the passing of the years. When he grew up the hero became an accountant, and accountants being notoriously sensitive, the story of his father's decease would periodically emerge to haunt him. When he fell in love, he did not know how to tell his intended of this skeleton in the family cupboard. On another occasion someone began a biography on his father and advertised for friends and relatives to come forward with helpful information.

Over the years, however, the hero hit upon a device to neutralise the story, one which above all would stop people laughing at the punch line. This was to tell the story truly and accurately, but boringly. The hero practised this to perfection – heavy circumstantial asides, a long digression on the domestic architecture of Naples, and a contrived prolixity.

It worked.

This story is a testimony to the power of boring people, and one of the easiest ways is to relay the obvious in the tone of the profound. Much of the literature on successful management is of this kind, replete with insights of the type that top managers have above average IQs and are more likely to come from middle-class than working-class homes. Rather than summarise this literature we will take a different approach and come to the question of the individual career success of managers via the notion of style. But what do we mean by management style? The question can be answered at different levels.

NATIONAL STYLE

To begin with an idea from the last two chapters, that of the differences between countries, it is probably fair to say that one can generalise across individual differences in various countries and point to broad-brush-stroke management styles which such countries exhibit. Take West Germany as an example.

Managers in that country are much less informal than American managers. They characteristically use Mr, Mrs (and Dr) forms of address, they seldom use Christian names, they keep their jackets on, their ties tight, and their shirt sleeves unrolled. They joke much less than their British counterparts and they swear a good deal less as well. When British managers participate in or chair meetings they seek to demonstrate their wit; when Germans take part in meetings they seek to demonstrate their serious-minded command of the business in hand.

It is sometimes said of Americans that they are, metaphorically at least, always selling something. The corresponding observation for Germans would be that they are always making something. Or to put it another way German management has a much stronger technical orientation than British or American management. Sales is not an especially high status function in German companies, marketing is not esteemed or even well understood as in American companies, but the technical functions in Germany have high standing. A higher proportion of German managers are engineers by training, and the typical top manager in Germany is an engineer as well. Problems and challenges in German companies are much more likely to be seen in technical terms; German managers aim at higher quality, better design, or superior after sales service in a simple and explicit way.

In the USA and Britain there is a generalist tradition. American managers think they can 'manage anything' and British managers are proud of being 'good all-rounders'. But German managers tend to see themselves as specialists, and if asked what they do will reply that they are designers or production controllers or export salesmen rather than use the general word manager. Consequently they tend to think of being qualified for particular posts in management much more in terms of relevant knowledge, especially where it is technical knowledge.

American managers understand the realities of power and British managers are (at least face to face) deferential in their dealings with superiors. German managers are more outspoken, more critical upwards, and more ready to indulge in the censure of others (if there is one thing a German likes more than a good moan it is a bit of righteous condemnation). There is no phrase in German for 'don't rock the boat' and they rock it all the time.

For anyone who thinks that perhaps the Germans are a special case, more sharply differentiated than other peoples, consider another country as an example of the national management style idea. This country is the fourth largest in Europe, yet its overall population is less than that of New York City or London – Sweden.

At first sight Sweden is like Germany. There is a strong engineering tradition, the same emphasis on design, and production, and right functioning. Yet there are differences. The Swedes are quietly efficient, in contradistinction to the Germans who are 'noisily efficient' or to the English who would not be seen dead labelled efficient.

The Swedes have a fantastic export tradition. In a way they

are not alone in this; the Germans are strong on exports and the Americans achieve quasi-exports everywhere with their manufacturing subsidiaries. So what is different about Swedish managers? It is the naturalness of their export-mindedness. They do not so much consciously strive for exports in the manner of the Germans as view them as a natural manifestation of business life. Swedish managers use expressions such as 'our home market is Scandinavia' (as opposed to Sweden) or 'exports are important to this company and that means selling outside Western Europe'.

Swedish managers are spectacularly egalitarian, in their dealings with the workforce and with each other. The 1976 Medbestämmende Lågen (Codetermination Act) gives Swedish employees the right to negotiate with management on pretty well anything they choose, which implies a good deal of manager–worker contact and compromise. Swedish, like French, is a language where there are two words for you, a polite form and an intimate form (Ni and Du respectively). It is a joke in Sweden that the only place where you will be addressed as Ni, the formal form, is at the SAS check-in counter at Arlander airport outside Stockholm. The first time I was introduced to the head of a Swedish company the name plate on his door bore the legend – Bill.

But the style is not merely informal and eglitarian. It is also madly reasonable. Swedish managers do not overwhelm you or charismatise you, they do not 'sell' you things or seek to dominate, they construct for you interpretations and courses of action which are unimpeachably reasonable and flow from quietly shared competences.

Again it follows that Swedish managers are not adversarial in their style. They have discussions rather than confrontations, they share information rather than articulate differences of opinion. There is less interdepartmental rivalry, less office warfare, less general skullduggery in Swedish companies than in their British or American equivalent. Swedish managers appear less secretive; the things they are talking about are the real agenda, not a cloak for a hidden agenda.[1]

In short, one can treat management style at a national level, characterise and differentiate, and point to strengths and weakness which derive from these style differences. But this is not the only option. Style may also be construed epochally, as the expression of a society in a time period.

MANAGEMENT STYLE AND THE AMERICAN SPIRIT

The USA in the 1950s is a good starting point for this idea that management style may be seen as epochal, rather than individual. According to the American psychologist David Riesman, by the 1950s Americans had become 'other directed'.[2]

To take a step back, Riesman discerns three modes of socialisation, where socialisation is the process whereby new members of some collectivity come to take over its values and socially acceptable practices. First we have tradition-directed man who is socialised by the clan, tribe, or village community. His behaviour is guided by adherence to detailed norms of village life learned by observation. Tradition-directed man inhabits pre-industrial, rural societies, and does not have anything to do with modern America. In economic terms tradition-directed man is oriented to subsistence.

Second, there is inner-directed man who is socialised by his parents. He adheres to general principles laid down early in his life, and feels guilty if he violates these. He is predisposed to work and achievement and economically speaking he is production oriented. Finally there is other-directed man who is socialised by his peer group, or the equals with whom he has contact. His behaviour is guided by his intuitive awareness of what others expect of him. He tends to be manipulative, and sensitive to status nuances. Economically he is consumption oriented.

The Riesman thesis is that the USA in the 1950s was peopled by other-directed human beings. They were not forceful individualists, but sensitive reactors. For them the group was reality, the individual an aberation. It was in this intellectual climate created by Riesman that a second influential book appeared, William Whyte's *Organisation Man.*[3] In Whyte's view the American business corporations of the

1950s represented the home *par excellence* of other-directed man.

In the same way that Riesman saw a transition from inner-directed man to other-directed man, Whyte plots a transition from the Protestant Ethic to the Social Ethic. The Protestant Ethic symbolises work, achievement, striving, self-discipline, and self-regulation. It is the ethos of nineteenth-century America, and, in terms of Whyte's personal experiences, of twentieth-century America until the post Second World War period as well. Then the Protestant Ethic was supplanted by the Social Ethic.

The crux of the matter is that the business corporation was the dominant organisation in the USA of the 1950s, and its dominance is increasing. To get on in these corporations one has to do what other people want. The successful people in the corporate society are corporate executives or people in similar large organisations. The point is that the way to success is not any more via private entreprise or individual achievement, via enterpreneurialism or initiative or the frontiersman spirit. This change, from individualism equals success to collectivism equals success, is at variance with the American Dream values of sturdy independence, log-cabin building, with the rail splitter to president tradition. Because the new collectivism of the corporations is at variance with the American Dream some other validating ideology is required, and this William Whyte calls the Social Ethic.

The Social Ethic is 'that contemporary body of thought which makes morally legitimate the pressures of society against the individual'.[4] It encompasses three beliefs: that the group is a source of creativity, that 'belongingness' is the ultimate need of the individual, and that science (certainly applied psychology) can be used to engineer belongingness.

What does this mean in practice? That for these 1950s executives amiability, compromise, tactfulness, and the desire to belong (to the corporation itself and to groups therein) were in, whereas independence, critical faculties, originality, innovation, leadership, and authority were out.

Furthermore these 'organisation men' sought to recruit, and perpetuate, the system in their own image and likeness.

According to Whyte they did this very effectively, drawing into these corporations of the 1950s mediocre but vocationally oriented graduates, who were both group conscious and security minded (at the selection interviews they asked more questions about retirement pensions than starting salaries). These acceding graduates tended to want staff jobs rather than the more exposed line positions in the companies they were joining. No one wanted to go into sales, for instance, since it is too aggressive and individualist, but everyone wanted to enter market research or become a 'merchandising specialist'.

In developing this thesis Whyte produced thumbnail sketches of the old thrusting American manager and the new organisation man and sent these off to samples of 150 corporation presidents and 150 personnel directors for comment. In fact half the presidents 'voted for' the old style manager, which no doubt reflected the fact that they were old style managers themselves, socialised in the Protestant Ethic as inner-directed men. More interesting was the response of the personnel directors; not only did the majority opt for the new-style organisation man, but they also gave Whyte their reasons with some force. The rough-and-tumble days of American industry were over, no more pioneering; unorthodoxy was undesirable; ideas came from the group not the individual; and creative leadership was a staff function. That is to say that if and when new ideas are needed these should be produced by specialised side-kicks but the organisation men will evaluate and implement them (painlessly!).

FROM THE LONELY CROWD TO THE GAMESMAN

With the benefit of hindsight one can see that Whyte captured some salient features of American society in the period concerned and worked out their implications for management style very cleverly. In this, like Riesman, he was very much part of an intellectual mood, part of a secure society's questioning of itself. At the same time he exaggerated his thesis, and wilfully ignored the pluses of group work and social sensitivity. Looking back it is difficult to reconcile

Whyte's highly critical account with the fact that the period was one of unparalleled business growth and profitability. Yet Whyte's book will always be of interest, not just to intellectual–social historians of the USA, but as the first powerful attempt to characterise the management style of a period. The first but not the last.

Twenty years later another American psychologist Michael Maccoby has taken up the story and produced a style characterisation of the American manager which does capture much of the reality of the late twentieth century.[5] In Maccoby's view there are four style types among the managers he studied and interviewed in several large high technology companies in the USA. These four types are the craftsman, the company man, the jungle fighter, and the modern gamesman: it is the last type, the gamesman, who is the predominant type.

The craftsman, Maccoby's first type, is not so much a craftsman in the manual sense as one seeking to develop and perfect systems in the electronics and telecommunications industry. In practice he will be a project leader or development engineer or R&D manager (not a woodcarver). The craftsman, in Maccoby's typology, is loyal to the organisation but not engulfed by it, managerially competent but not very political, and his mainspring is a passion for doing technical things well, for developing something better. In David Riesman's terms he is more inner directed: in William Whyte's terms he is not an organisation man, but someone on a parallel track.

Maccoby's company man, however, is William Whyte's organisation man 20 years on. In reading Maccoby's characterisation of the company man this seems to be almost literally true, where the company man is described as being in his fifties, near the top but never at the top. He is courteous and dignified, very loyal to the corporation and the social ethics he ascribes to it, but without enough 'get up and go' to get to the top in the modern competitive milieu.

The jungle fighter is a familiar type. He is simply power-crazed, with undertones of paranoia. He wants to amass power, and to dominate. He deals in terms of accomplices rather than colleagues, and is likely to fail where team work is needed, especially team work to achieve some creative purpose.

The gamesman is the dominant type and increasingly the shape of things to come. The gamesman is the professional. He is fast, flexible, loves change, and is in it to win. This winning is the real motivation. The gamesman is not seeking power *per se* even though additional increments of power will be his whenever he wins. Neither is he in any direct or simple sense a materialist. He expects a high income and an affluent life style, but these will serve primarily to assure him that he is winning, that he is 'earning up to his age' or maybe 'gotten ahead for his age grade'. But the wealth is secondary, for the gamesman lives to work (and win) not works to spend.

The gamesman thrives in the high technology industries where the pace of change is fastest and where need for intrinsic cleverness is greatest. The gamesman is an educated manager, usually scientifically educated. He needs to understand the technology, to know what the craftsmen of Maccoby's typology are striving to create, and be able to help them intellectually as well as organisationally.

The gamesman can work through people. He has social skills, can sell himself, sell ideas, and motivate others. He is emotionally controlled: he can stand the pace, cope with being put down by his boss from time to time, and keep on playing. Maccoby is impressed by the gamesman. Gamesmen get things done, difficult things, creative things, things involving myriads of others. Yet at the same time Maccoby does not like (or trust) the gamesman. He finds the commitment to winning a bit clinical, a little amoral, and is worried by the fact that the gamesmen themselves are not worried about the products their companies manufacture and the uses to which these may be put.

Maccoby has provided an answer to the question: what is the style of the modern American manager? In doing this he has not only built on the Riesman and Whyte ideas of an earlier decade, but pointed the way ahead as well. It is implicit in the Maccoby analysis that gamesmen are on the way in and up. For the moment their prime location is in the high technology industries but like the Jomsberg Vikings they will go forth and conquer other lands with their skills and energy. In 10 years' time stuffy old industries like ship-building and steel will have either disappeared, or been revitalised – by gamesmen on the make.

MANAGEMENT STYLE AND INDIVIDUAL CHOICE

If we look at management style at the individual rather than national or epochal level it is fair to ask: is it the product of individual choice; le style, est-ce que l'enfant de la liberté?

There is not a straight answer. Individual style appears to be an amalgam of personal choice on the one hand and personality and culture on the other. Most of the literature is about the latter but the present purpose is to repeat, and underline, the fact that management jobs usually afford some choice.

This idea of the choice inherent in management work was developed in chapter 3 using ideas from Rosemary Stewart's book *Choices for the Manager.*[6] She has shown very persuasively that managers can often choose to emphasise, say, the technical or the supervisory nature of their jobs, vary the amount of contact with subordinates and bosses, put more or less emphasis on boundary maintenance, take up variable stances on risk and innovation, and so on. To underline the idea it might be helpful to give a practical example of this choice in action.

I once made a time budget analysis of the work of sixteen

Table 8.1

Type of activity	Proportion of time (%)
Meetings	43
Touring the works	17
Telephoning	11
Desk work	12

managers, that is made a note of all the things they did during a 2-day work period so that one could classify these activities and work out average proportions of time spent on them.[7] It emerged that four categories of activity – meetings formal and informal, tours of the works, telephoning, and desk work – accounted for over 80% of their working time. The breakdown is shown in Table 8.1. But this is just to give the average results for the small sample. Within that group of sixteen managers there were marked differences in the proportions of time that could be categorised as shown in Table 8.2.

Table 8.2

Type of activity	Highest proportion of time scored by any one manager (%)	Lowest proportion of time scored by any one manager (%)
Meetings	81	5
Tour of the works	42	0
Telephoning	25	1
Desk work	22	5

In short the variations are enormous. But there were only sixteen managers in the sample, they were all Germans, all production managers doing comparable jobs, and the study was accomplished over a short time period. Management work permits some choice.

DIMENSIONS OF STYLE

It is one of the peculiarities of social science research that there is not much in the way of studies of individual management style but lots of research on leadership styles. Clearly the two are connected, in the sense that much of the work of many managers does come under the heading of leadership, but still management and leadership are not synonyms. First this is because different management jobs vary in the extent to which they require leadership qualities, and there are time and place differences as well. And second most managers do, and are required to do, other things that do not come under the heading of leadership. With this qualification three principal dimensions of (leadership) style emerge from the many studies.[8]

The first dimension is variously known as initiating structure, production orientation, or task centredness. This dimension is all about getting the job done. It covers leadership activities such as defining the situation, specifying objectives, elaborating means for their achievement, overcoming technical or situational obstacles to task achievement, breaking down the task and assigning particular jobs to subordinates, controlling progress and monitoring results. Managers/leaders differ in their facility and inclination for all this; they exhibit different degrees of task centredness.

The second dimension is alternative and compensatory and it is variously known as consideration, people centredness, concern for people. This concern for people on the part of the manager/leader covers relating to people as people, being concerned with their welfare and problems, wanting them to like you and respond to you, seeking to maintain morale and enhance group cohesion.

These first two dimensions of task centredness and people centredness have been combined by Blake and Mouton into a grid (Fig. 8.1). These researchers have, that is, constructed a questionnaire, and from answers to the questionnaire items managers or supervisors taking the test can be scored 1–9 on the two dimensions.[9] So the vertical axis of the grid represents people centredness with the 1 at the bottom and the 9 at the top, and the horizontal axis represents task centredness with the 1 on the left and the 9 on the right. This grid enables individuals taking the test to be scored in any of the 81 boxes or interstices of the grid according to their performance on each of the two dimensions. Thus any individual scoring 1.1 is a poor performer on both dimensions of leadership, whereas someone scoring 9.9 is brilliant (of which more later). On the other hand, someone scoring 1.9 is strong on people and weak on task and this is dubbed 'country-club management', whereas someone scoring 9.1 is strong on task but weak on concern for people ('task management').

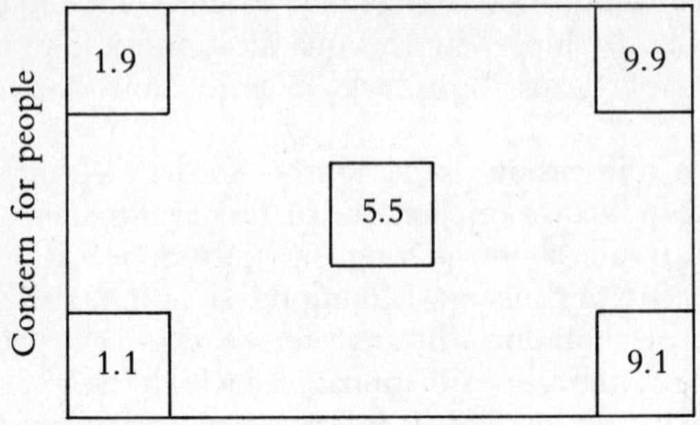

Figure 8.1

The third dimension of leadership style is participation. This covers the extent to which the manager/leader involves subordinates in decisions. In practice there are all sorts of variations. The manager may for instance:

— make a decision on his own and not even tell subordinates
— make a decision and tell them afterwards
— ask their opinion and then make the decision
— make the decision with the subordinates in a group meeting
— delegate the making of the decision to the subordinates and let them tell him
— let them do it their way keep it to themselves!

This is the nature of the participation dimension, though in practice it is more diffuse than this pure decision grading suggests.

These three dimensions can be varied in degree and combination. Some players can even vary the style to suit the occasion, as Maccoby's gamesmen would tell you. So the critical question is: what are they good for? What leadership styles are presumed to get results in which situations?

There is a lot of research on this, but the findings are not clear cut, with one study tending to undermine another or qualify its findings. A few generalisations, however, are possible. Let us start with task-centred leadership.

Task-centred leadership is presumed to impose a structure on the task in hand. If, however, the task is naturally structured anyway task-centred leadership tends to have an alienating effect on subordinates. The same applies to repetition. The combination of task-centred leadership and a repetitive task is also alienating for subordinates. On the other hand if the task is naturally unstructured then task-centred leadership tends to raise the satisfaction and performance of subordinates. Danger has the same effect. There are, that is, studies from combat situations which suggests that those involved in dangerous tasks prefer task-centred leaders, presumably in the expectation that the task-centred leader is most likely to get it right and get them back alive. And finally subordinates who have authoritarian leanings like task-centred leadership irrespective of how dangerous or unstructured is the task.

People-centred leadership, we will call it supportive leadership, tends to be effective with tasks that are stressful, frustrating, or dissatisfying. In such cases supportive leadership may raise the subordinates' self-confidence and underline for them the importance of their contribution with positive effects on morale. Again if the task is highly structured (boring, repetitive, little room for manoeuvre or the expression of personal style) then supportive leadership is likely to raise satisfaction and performance (nothing else can!).

There are a number of reasons for believing that participative leadership is likely to raise the satisfaction and performance of subordinates, it is not just a question of preferring it on ethical-democratic grounds. First, participative leadership means that subordinates will be better informed; after all, they are more directly involved in making the decisions. Being well-informed may embrace an understanding of which task-related behaviours are directly rewarded ('They say we have to do this, this, and this but what do they really want?'). Second, participative leadership may enable subordinates to choose goals which directly reflect the amount of effort they are prepared to expend; that is, better understanding enables them to get the effort-reward equation right. Third, participative leadership may enable subordinates to choose goals to which they are attached and they will then presumptively strive harder to achieve them. Fourth, participative leadership by definition means that subordinates have enhanced control over their work and this is usually associated with working harder.

To these bits of reasoning two further operating premises may be added. If a task is both unstructured and ego-involving (the subordinate identifies with it) participative leadership raises the subordinates' job satisfaction. And irrespective of the nature of the task, participative leadership will get the best out of people who have strong independence and self-direction drives.

There is a further derivative of the people-oriented or supportive style. This is manifest in setting high performance standards for subordinates and taking trouble to convince them that they are capable of achieving these standards. We will call this achievement oriented leadership. The idea is that this will encourage subordinates to strive for higher standards and have more confidence in their ability to meet challenging goals. There is evidence that this achievement-oriented style pays off where subordinates are working on non-repetitive and ambiguous tasks.

SUCCESS: STYLE AND CONVICTIONS

The discipline of organisational behaviour has thrown up a lot of theories of motivation and job satisfaction, and a study in the late 1970s has shown that many of these relate directly to the career success of individual managers.[10] This key study is known as the Achieving Manager Research Project and its authors are two Americans, Jay Hall and Susan Donnell. The gist of this study is that the researchers have taken some 12000 managers, graded them objectively as to high, medium, or low career success, and then cross-tabulated their career-success level with their scores on a variety of tests and questionnaires which highlight their style, attitudes, and opinions. An assessment of the practices of these managers by their subordinates has also been built into the research design. It is a very fruitful study.

The measure of managerial achievement on which the whole thing is based is a modified version of an instrument known as the Managerial Achievement Quotient developed by Dr Benjamin Rhodes. This instrument: 'affords an evaluation of an individuals's career progress in the light of his chronological age, taking into account the number of career moves necessary to reach the top of a typical organisation and the age span most germane to career planning'.[11]

First of all it emerges from the study that the career-successful managers hold a different 'cosmology' of management. In 1960 an American writer, Douglas McGregor, produced a famous book *The Human Side of Enterprise*[12] in which he postulated two views of man and motivation which he called Theory X and Theory Y. Theory X holds that man is basically idle and selfish and can only be motivated to do anything by cash rewards crossed with a substantial dollop of supervision. Theory Y, on the other hand, posits that man is capable of working for intrinsic satisfactions and of accepting even higher levels of satisfaction, especially if trusted. The study showed a marked tendency for the low-achieving managers to hold Theory X views. Success, in other words, is on the side of the enlightened.

Next it emerged that the successful managers have a different motivation profile. Hall and Donnell used what is called the Work Motivation Inventory which is designed to assess the factors most important to an individual in work-related situations. This inventory generates five scores indicating the importance the individual manager attaches to basic creature comfort, safety, belongingness, ego-status, and self-actualisation or self-fulfilment. The results were unambiguous. The need for self-realisation is the dominant motivational influence for the high-achieving managers; the average achievers are mostly driven by ego-status needs (the need to look good, to be seen to have 'made it'); and the low achievers and preoccupied with creature comfort and ego-status needs. In short what the individual manager achieves is conditioned by why he wants to achieve it.

The discipline of organisational behaviour, in analysing the determinants of job satisfaction, distinguishes between what are called hygiene factors and motivators. Hygiene factors are aspects of the job which are negatively important in the sense that people will be dissatisfied if they do not have them but will not be positively motivated by having them. In practice the term covers things like working conditions and pay. Motivators, on the other hand, are the things that positively motivate – sense of satisfaction, recognition, praise, sense of real achievement, and so on. A third finding of the Hall and Donnell study is that high-achieving managers place a lot of emphasis on these motivator factors – realisation of potential, belonging, ego-status considerations – in their treatment of their subordinates. Low-achieving managers, on the other hand, concentrate on the hygiene factors in their handling of subordinates. A successful manager stresses the right things for those he manages.

The Hall and Donnell study also confirms our earlier speculations on the putative merits of participative leadership. 'High Achievers are reported (i.e. by the people who work for them) to employ participative practices to such a greater extent that participative management may be said to be a major characteristic of the High-Achieving Group.'[13]

Another major finding of the study is that the successful managers have a superior interpersonal competence where the latter is understood in terms of:

— accepting responsibility for one's own ideas and attitudes
— being open to the ideas of others
— experimenting with new ideas and attitudes
— helping and encouraging others to do all these things.

The level of interpersonal competence in these senses seems to be directly related to high achievement, this again being confirmed by the people who work for the successful managers.

Finally the managers were tested on a variation of the Blake and Mouton grid, discussed earlier in the chapter, which measures leadership style on the dimensions of concern for people and concern for task. The result is quite fascinating. The low-achievers have low scores on both dimensions, the average achievers have high scores on the task orientation but still a low score on the people orientation, and the high-achieving managers have high scores on both. In other words concern for the task will get you from poor to average, but you need concern for people to get from average to good. Or in simple Blake and Mouton terms being a 9.9 really makes you top.

SUCCESS: BACKGROUND AND ATTRIBUTES

In discussing the real work of managers in chapter 2 we left out the most recent study in this tradition. It is the work of a Harvard Business School Professor, John Kotter, and is a quite magnificent study of the work of fifteen high-level general managers in several American companies.[14] Kotter studied his chosen managers by interviewing them, observing them at work, interviewing their subordinates, getting them to do some tests, and collecting background information on them. His sample is small, but by definition they are all highly successful, having reached the upper levels of substantial companies. What do Kotter's managers have in common? A good deal as it turns out.

In background terms they are connected not so much by middle-class origins as by having upwardly mobile parents. They have come from stable homes with both the original parents being at home while the manager-as-child was growing up. The managers in the sample indeed claimed a close relationship with one or both of their parents. They tended to have fathers who were associated with business, or at least working as managers in a non-business setting. Perhaps surprisingly in view of all the studies of the connection between achievement and 'lonely-only' children, this group of managers all had brothers and sisters.

All fifteen managers had been to university, and several of them had masters as well as first degrees. All their qualifications were in business related subjects. What is more all of them had been student leaders in high school or college.

The group are also connected by certain early career experiences. They all joined a firm or industry that fitted closely with their personal interests and values, and stayed with it. In short most of them had spent most of their career in one industry, and indeed with one employer. They had also risen through one function (in the sense of Marketing or R&D or Personnel) or at the most two. It is interesting that they were much less mobile sideways – between functions, firms, or industries – than some of the folklore about managerial advancement suggests is desirable.

Their basic personalities also showed some interesting uniformities. These managers liked power, liked achievement, and were openly ambitious: clearly they had not had 'greatness thrust upon them' but had gone looking for it. They also emerged as emotionally stable, and indeed optimistic – prophecies of doom, however well founded, will not get you to the top!

The group are all clever (above average intelligence) without being brilliant; they are quite strong in terms of analytic abilities and very strong intuitively – good judgement, able to assess people, sensitive to situations, reliable 'gut feelings'. As per Hall and Donnell they showed strong interpersonal skills being personable, good at relationship building, and having a range of interests that enabled them to relate to lots of different groups of people.

Furthermore Kotter argues that they developed in certain ways during their careers. Firstly they became very knowledgeable about the business they were in – banking, electronics, or whatever – and secondly they became very well-informed about the particular organisation in which they worked. These two knowledge accumulations were paralleled by relationship developments. That is to say, they successfully developed relationships with large numbers of people both within their organisation and in the industry, so that by the time they became general managers they already had extensive networks.

If we cross these two studies a clear picture of the successful manager emerges. High-minded, liberal, open, and participative on the one hand, and on the other stable, ambitious, personable, and above all relevantly knowledgeable in every way. In the next and last chapter we will see what social-science research has to say about the success of companies rather than individuals.

NOTES

1 Readers who would like to know more about Sweden are referred to: Peter Lawrence and Tony Spybey (1986) *Management and Society in Sweden*, Routledge & Kegan Paul, London.

2 David Riesman *et al.* (1950) *The Lonely Crowd*, Yale University Press, New Haven.

3 William H. Whyte (1956) *The Organisation Man*, Simon & Schuster, New York.

4 Ibid., p. 12.

5 Michael Maccoby (1978) *The Gamesman*, Bantam Books, New York.

6 Rosemary Stewart (1982) *Choices for the Manager*, McGraw Hill, Maidenhead, Berkshire.

7 The details of this time subject analysis are to be found in: S. P. Hutton and P. A. Lawrence (1979) *The Work of Production Managers: Case Studies at Manufacturing Companies in West Germany*, Report to the Department of Industry, London; also available from the University of Loughborough Library.

8 R. R. Blake and J. S. Mouton (1964) *The Management Grid*, Gulf Publisher, Houston.

9 For a good discussion of leadership theories and supporting research evidence see Alan Bryman (1986) *Leadership & Organisation*, Routledge & Kegan Paul, London.

10 Jay Hall and Susan M. Donnell (1979) Managerial achievement: The personal side of behavioural theory, *Human Relations*, **32**, 1, 77–101.

11 Ibid., p. 81.
12 Douglas McGregor (1960) *The Human Side of Enterprise*, McGraw Hill, New York.
13 Hall & Donnell op. cit., p. 92.
14 John P. Kotter (1982) *The General Managers*, The Free Press, New York.

9

The Success of Companies

In a generally complicated world there is at least one simple verity: profit is the hallmark of successful companies.

Or is it? The proposition does have common-sense support, it is a convention in the business world, and it does permit the measuring of success, quantifying it, and making comparisons between companies; and all that is a good deal. So the contention deserves to be taken seriously, though it is subject to three sets of qualifications.

The first is about values and personal choice. One may hold that other things are more important than profit, even in a free enterprise, capitalist society. So that it may be argued that companies which spurn, say, the values of environmentalism, or individualism, or the common man's right to work, or whatever, cannot be deemed successful no matter how impressively they perform on criteria of profitability. This really is a matter of individual choice rather than economic theory.

The second qualification is more down to earth but less publicly canvassed than the issue of competing social values. It is quite simply that there is nothing absolute about profit, its definition or measurement. The starting point is that companies do not make profits in eternity but by finite time period. One speaks of trading profits per year, or quarter, not per company lifetime. And the amount of profit a given company is deemed to have made in, say, 1990 is not in any simple way a unique reflection of its business performance but the product of accounting conventions and variable practice. To give one common example, how and above all when one writes off depreciating plant and machinery may make a big difference to the declared profit for any one year. How one values stock-in-hand (completed but unsold manufactures) may also affect the profit for any period. So may the terms on which borrowings are repaid. In other words, the profit that is shown in official statements for companies is the product of accountancy practice; it does relate to reality but not in a unique or unvarying way.

The third qualification is that profit is relative. It is relative to the scale of operations, the effort that goes into the enterprise, the capital employed. Making a profit is not enough, it has to be a profit in proportion to the endeavour. Consider two deliberately absurd examples. If General Motors made a profit of $100 000 in a given trading year this would be tantamount to bankruptcy. But if the drug store in Wall, South Dakota, made $100 000 in a year it would be doing superbly well.

To take this relative argument a little further, a company's profitability, rather than its profit, is investigated in terms of various financial ratios. So that one is interested in, say, the profit to equity ratio, or earnings per share. Or one focuses on the ratio between profit and capital employed, or the profits to sales ratio, or looks at the way the company has increased its assets or value over time.

In short, two views are being urged. First, that profit is important as a criterion of company success, but it is not the simple and absolute arbiter which it is often depicted as being. Second, that profitability, rather than profit, is what counts, though profitability is also no simple absolute, but an abstact and variable entity apprehended by means of 'ratio analysis'. If then we have these more discriminating measures of corporate success in the form of various financial performance criteria, the next question is simply what makes companies succeed?

From the 1950s on, organisational sociology has thrown up a number of hypotheses about corporate success, variously centring on size, structure, and environment, and the relations between them. Let us start with an easy one, size.

BIGNESS BEATS ALL

In popular usage bureaucracy denotes slowness, inefficiency, and arid impersonality, but it is important to realise that these pejorative connotations are relatively recent. Viewed historically, bureaucracy in the sense of the rational division of tasks, employment of well-trained administrators, and orderly procedures, was a great advance on what preceded it – favouritism, amateurism, and despotism. Bureaucracy actually means having rules and procedures in the interests of efficiency, giving appropriate specialist training to administrators, and being even-handed in the treatment of individual cases. This is the (neglected) case for bureaucracy.

It is relevant to a discussion of the success of companies because small companies tend not to be bureaucratic and, *ipso facto*, not to enjoy the efficiency benefits of bureaucracy. Bigness and bureaucracy may not be fashionable but this should not blind us to their strengths.

There are some things that these big and bureaucratic companies do superbly well. In general terms their strengths tend to be financial planning and control; anything to do with costs, budgets, and allocations. These large bureaucratic companies are also often impressive in terms of their personnel policies – recruitment procedures, abundant training, performance appraisal, management development, and thought through remuneration packages. These things may not sound exciting but they have a lot to do with the effective accomplishment of big tasks by large numbers of people. So the syllogism for the present discussion is that bigness facilitates bureaucracy which correlates with efficiency which is a determinant of success. There are two variations on this theme.

The first is that increased size is associated with a higher level of what is known as 'structural differentiation'. Structural differentiation is where the organisation generates additional structural entities for new or more specialised tasks. Or in more homely language, the bigger a company gets the more likely it is to have various specialist departments. Indeed we have explored this idea already in chapter 3 in the discussion of the various departments or functions which go to make up business firms, and in chapter 5 with the contrasted account of the small business.

Just to recap, in smaller companies many functions, including production engineering, maintenance, production control, and purchasing, are organisationally integrated with production; they are, that is, subsections of production, reporting to production managers. Indeed in very small companies even quality control (inspection) may be part of the 'production empire'. But as the size of firm increases so does the tendency for these production-related functions to be 'separated out', to become independent, separate departments.

Or again, very small firms, as argued in chapter 5, have no management team, no specialisation among managers. Small firms do not have personnel departments, and do not discharge marketing functions, only sales. Only large firms have R&D, or management-services departments. In other words both the degree of specialisation and the range of competences increase with size.

The second variation on the theme concerns impersonality and decentralisation, though this idea is admittedly more speculative. The argument goes like this. A small business may be heavily centralised and the managing director may exercise a strong personal control. But this set up is difficult to achieve in large firms. So large firms tend to develop more impersonal means of control and decentralised structures. So what? Well, it is at this stage that the argument becomes more speculative, but there is a school of thought which says that impersonal controls are less likely to alienate those who are subject to them, that the very impersonality takes the sting out of compliance. It becomes a matter of achieving targets rather than of 'doing what the man says'. And decentralisation? Well it has been argued that decentralisation is good for initiative and local autonomy, for proper focus and for performance measurement.[1] But this appraisal of decentralisation leads away from the notion of size and into that of structure, and there are several theories that relate corporate success to organisational structure.

TECHNOLOGY STRUCTURE AND SUCCESS

One of the most influential of these theories serving to explain the success of companies in terms of their organisational structure is the work of the English sociologist Joan Woodward.[2] The input for her study is a mass of information for over a hundred firms in south-east Essex, information based on an analysis of the structure, composition of the workforce, and the administrative procedures of the companies.[3]

With the benefit of hindsight the Woodward thesis can be reconstructed in four stages. First there are three broad types of production technology: unit production (or small batch), mass production (or large batch), and process production. Unit or small-batch production is where things are made singly or in small numbers, for instance bespoke tailored suits, battleships, or power stations. The underlying idea is that there will be a lot of variety among the company's products in response to customer demand. Small batch does not mean the company does not make many things, it means it does not make many the same. Mass production is the volume production of a small range of highly standardised products, typically using a high level of division of labour and mechanisation: cars are always given as the archetypal example. And process production is where the output is dimensional rather than integral, where you measure it rather than count it (the distinction propounded in chapter 3). Thus examples of process industry are chemicals, pharmaceuticals, oil refineries, breweries, and food-processing companies. Stage one then is the designation of these three broad production technologies – unit, mass, and process.

Stage two is the assembling of a mass of information about the sample of a hundred or more companies. The effect of this operation is to show that they vary massively in structural, manpower, and procedural ways; that differences do not seem to form any kind of pattern, and they are not explained by size.

Stage three is the categorisation of the firms in the sample in terms of the unit–mass–process-production typology. When this is done all the differences fall into place and a strong pattern emerges. If one takes, for example, the variables of the number of ranks in the organisational hierarchy, the ratio of managers to workers, the ratio of direct to indirect labour (production workers are direct labour, everyone else is indirect), and the proportion of university graduates involved in the organisation of production, then these are all low for unit-production firms, medium for mass-production firms, and high for process-production firms. So to take the strong end of the scale the typical process-production firm has a long hierarchy, high proportions of managers, indirect labour, and graduates. Or again, if one takes the variables of, say, the span of control of the foremen (the number of workers they oversee), the degree of inflexibility in the organisation, the amount of written as opposed to verbal communication, and the separation of technical from managerial functions, then these are relatively low in unit-production firms, become high in mass-production firms, and revert to being low in process-production firms. Again, to take the strong example, the typical mass-production firm has foremen who supervise large numbers of workers, it is relatively inflexible, it exhibits a preference for written rather than verbal communication, and the technical specialists are kept separate from the managers to a higher degree than in the firms of the other two types. So to sum up, stage three gives us companies which are patterned structurally and in other ways according to whether they are unit, mass, or process production.

Stage four is engagingly simple. When Woodward reclassified the firms according to success and performance, it emerged that the most successful ones were those which were *closest to the norm* for their type. The most successful mass-production firms, for example, were those which were *typical* mass production in terms of all the variables mentioned above.

In other words, it is not simply a case of unit-production firms 'just happening' to be like this, and mass production firms 'just happening' to be like that, but rather that they ought to conform to these models, and the more they do the more successful they are likely to be, other things being equal. This formula actually yields quite a lot of success pointers, so that if, for instance, you are running a process firm and you want corporate success, you should make sure it has an organisational structure in the form of a tall, slender pyramid (this is what many ranks in the hierarchy crossed with narrow spans of control gives you), that you employ lots of managers, lots of graduates, lots of indirect labour, are organisationally flexible and make the most of verbal communication.

CORPORATE SUCCESS AND THE BATTLE OF BRITAIN

The battle between the RAF and the Luftwaffe in August–September 1940 which prevented a German invasion of Britain is understandably written down a little bit by the Germans who call it not the Battle of Britain but the Battle of England (die Schlacht um England), and even more by the French who call it the Battle of London (la bataille de Londres). So perhaps it is in the spirit of this 'national inflation' that there is a theory of corporate success which takes the Battle of Britain as its starting point.

It is generally agreed that the key to British victory was the fact that we had a radar system (and the Germans did not) and could therefore plot incoming attack aircraft and deploy accordingly, making tactical gains from concentrating resources. In an influential book in the 1960s Burns and Stalker[4] argue that the critical factor in developing radar in Britain was the free flow of ideas and information between the research scientists, Air Ministry officials, and Air Force officers, a triumph of democracy and flexibility. The Germans, on the other hand, were both slow to appreciate the importance of radar and to develop it. They went about it in a more formal and impersonal way with little contact between the interested parties; in other words, they fouled it up with heavy-handed bureaucracy!

This contrast is an inspiration for Burns and Stalker. It provides the germ of an idea which they carry over to the study of a number of firms in, or entering, the electronics industry in the late 1950s. They look at the features of these firms, the situation they are in, and their effectiveness. All this leads them to posit the idea of two types of organisational structure which they call mechanistic and organic.[5]

In the mechanistic structure the managers have clearly defined tasks, with properly delimited authority. Hierarchy is important, and the higher up a manager is the more information he has. Indeed it is the vertical lines of communication which matter with orders coming down and information passing up. This mechanistic structure, Burns and Stalker argue, is appropriate for companies operating in a stable environment. It suits companies making familiar products by known methods and selling them in established markets.

The organic structure, on the other hand, is the reverse of all this. Managers in the organic structure may have tasks and competences that are only loosely defined; the top manager is not expected to be omniscient. But above all managers in the organic structure communicate, not just upwards and downwards, but sideways and diagonally as well. They communicate verbally, informally, enthusiastically. And the organic structure is appropriate for companies operating in a changing environment. It suits companies who seek to develop new products, work with new technologies, and sell in new markets.

In short, this is another theory of corporate success. It links organisational structure to business success via the medium of the environment. If the environment is stable à la Burns and Stalker, then the company ought to have a mechanistic structure; there will be attendant gains in reliability and efficiency and the concentration of effort. But if the environment changes, if new products, technologies, or markets become the order of the day then the company should develop an organic structure. Only an organic structure will have the flexibility and ideas flow to adapt, to make a success of the challenge, and it is important that this flexibility is not stifled by inappropriate structures.

The argument is particularly subtle for two opposed reasons. First there is a general conviction that the business environment is becoming more challenging, that the rate of change is increasing, and thus more companies have need of an organic structure to respond. On the other hand, it is clear from Burns and Stalker's research that companies which should, in their own interests, develop an organic structure do not always do so. The emergence of more flexible and less hierarchic ways of doing things may be frustrated by managers who feel the change would lose them status and influence.

THE ANSWER IN A CARDBOARD BOX

Perhaps the most sophisticated of these theories linking product, technology, structure, and markets on the one side with corporate success on the other is the work of the American academics Lawrence and Lorsch.[6] They work with two key variables, differentiation and integration.

Differentiation is the extent to which a company is broken down into separate functions, departments, or sections, divided up into specialised subunits. It is the idea of specialisation reviewed earlier in this chapter in discussing the effects of organisational size. The thing to add at this point is that differentiation is not only a refined concept, it is refined in practice as well. So that whether or not a company is big enough, differentiated enough, or responsible enough to have, say, a personnel department, is an example of differentiation. But one may take it further and compare companies which do have personnel departments. A company whose personnel department includes subsections or specialists in recruitment, training, remuneration packages, personnel planning, and management development is more differentiated than another company whose personnel department simply administers sickness benefits.[7] This is what Lawrence and Lorsch mean by differentiation.

Integration is the other half of the organisational equation, the response called forth by the challenge of differentiation. Integration is putting it all back together again, or more formally, recombining the contributions of these various specialised departments for the successful achievement of company objectives. In the conceptual vocabulary of Lawrence and Lorsch integration is both a process, the way in which these specialised subsections of the organisation are brought together, and a quality, or a level of cooperation among the organisation's different parts.

Integration is achieved in a variety of ways, the most common being the authority hierarchy, in which general managers integrate the contributions of various departments and 'the man at the top' integrates it all. At the same time it has to be said that the authority hierarchy as a mechanism for integration works better in theory than in practice! In practice, the would-be integrating higher managers may well find themselves confronted by genuine differences of interest among their subordinates, not mere factionalism, and have real difficulty knowing whom or what they should support – never mind implementing such awful decisions.[8]

Other ways in which this integration may be achieved are by consultation and participation, by joint committees, cross departmental teams and task forces, and by an initiating department involving others at critical points in the sequence, even if not continuously. Formal management education, in-company training, rotating managers between assignments in different departments, putting in individuals in a liaison role, even lending them short term to another department to give them an appreciation of its operating requirements and world view, are all resources for achieving good integration.

Using these two ideas of differentiation and integration Lawrence and Lorsch carried out a fascinating study of a small group of American firms in the 1960s. They chose firms from three industries – plastics, food-packaging, and containers (cardboard boxes). These three industries represent three levels of exposure to environmental uncertainty, high in the case of the plastics firms, medium for food packaging, low for containers. To unpack this proposition a little, the plastics companies were operating with a relatively new product and technology (as of the 1960s), price competition in the industry was fierce, there was a growing market and a lot of scope for product innovation. But all these things applied less to the food-packaging companies, and less still to the container companies operating with a stable product in an established but not expanding market.

The second twist to the Lawrence and Lorsch sample is to match successful and unsuccessful firms in each of the three industry groups. Success here is defined in terms of profit, sales, and product innovation (producing good new products). The study reveals a simple thing that 'everyone knows' and something less obvious with subtle ramifications. The simple thing is that the successful companies in all three industries were all good at integration. Never mind how they did it, it is clear that they did it, and they all end up with high scores on integration. In other words they are effectively drawing together the contributions from various parts of the company in the cause of achieving objectives. Success goes to those who can get the act together.

The less obvious thing is that the level of differentiation is different for the three industries. The container companies were least differentiated, the food-packaging firms were medium on differentiation, and the plastics firms were most highly differentiated. In other words the level of differentiation follows the level of environmental uncertainty. Stable environment means low differentiation, but unstable, challenging, uncertain environment means high differentiation, or in practical terms the development of various specialist units to cope with, respond to, or exploit, the opportunities of the environment. And if we join the two propositions together we get a conditional one. This is that successful companies have to be good at integration, but integration is more demanding for companies in an uncertain environment because they are more differentiated in the first place.

THE STRATEGIC CHOICE ARGUMENT

All the theories and propositions canvassed so far have something to say about corporate success, yet none claim to be comprehensive. They are conditional or contingent explanations. Lawrence and Lorsch, for instance, are saying implicitly: You want to be a successful company? First tell us what industry you are in, how uncertain is the environment, and then we can tell you how you have to stack up in terms of differentiation and integration. The fact that these theories do deal only in contingencies is a possible limitation, but another is their impersonality.

These theories, that is, postulate an impersonal relationship between the entities of product, market, environment, structure, and so on, without identifiable people actually doing things or deciding things. Just to burlesque it a little, we have, say, a stable environment à la Burns and Stalker. Then it becomes unstable; business organisations relating to it conscientiously develop organic structures, and then they do well. But where are the people who made it all happen?[9]

The argument can be reformulated by saying that the theories examined so far may well be right, but the dynamic relationships they posit will not actually occur unless and until people in those organisations decide to initiate change. What is more, the reference is not to 'people' at random, but to top people, powerful people, the top management team or 'the dominant coalition' as it is sometimes called. And if the decisive thing is what powerful people in the organisation want, their definition of success and ways of achieving it, then there is a case for moving the spotlight away from impersonal environment-structure linkages and on to corporate strategy, or the sets of strategic choices made by these senior management.

CORPORATE STRATEGY

Corporate strategy is the name given to this formulation of

middle-term company objectives and ways of achieving them, worked out by top managers and their corporate advisers. Corporate strategy is the sum of the strategic decisions and the state of affairs they are intended to bring about.[10] But what is a strategic decision, and how does it differ from other decisions made in business life?

Before answering the question directly it may be helpful to take a step back and consider the continuity of companies. The general public tend to have a touchingly simple view of the sameness and persistence of business enterprises. There is this sewing machine company, in the popular view, around for a long time and always in the same line of business. But in practice, there are a number of forces for change, of which the most important are invention, changes in taste or need, and changes over time in the profitability of particular operations.

Invention is perhaps the most straightforward. Inventions made new products and new industries possible. There was no aircraft industry in the nineteenth century, no plastics industry until certain developments in inorganic chemistry made plastics possible, IBM used to be the world's largest typewriter maker and is now the world's largest computer manufacturer.

But it is not just that invention brings in the new, side by side with the old: there is also succession, displacement, and reordering. Horse-drawn carriages were driven out by the Ford Model T; the availability of ball-point, felt-tip, and ball-liner pens has made the use of fountain pens almost fetishistic; only the Third World installs electro-mechanical (as opposed to electronic) telephone exchanges.

There is a problem about changes in taste and need, which is that one is never sure whether they have 'grown up naturally' or been fashioned by availability and commercial advocacy, but there is no doubt that the changes occur. In Britain today, for example, there is more demand for health foods, private education, Mediterranean package holidays, credit at gas stations, convenience foods, and tape recorder/cassette players than there was 10 years ago. But there is less demand for draught beer, asbestos sheeting, skate boards, TVs, cigarettes, clockwork watches, and white bread.

Nor is this phenomenon of taste and need change restricted to the preferences of the general public as consumers, even if they provide the most readily acceptable examples. In industrial buying – the purchase of components, materials, equipment, and so on – one can see changes in the direction of buyers wanting higher quality, more precision, shorter manufacturing lead times, and more favourable credit terms.

Changes in profitablity derive from the two things already discussed – technical change which makes things cheaper or dearer, and changes in taste and need which enlarge and depress markets for particular goods and services. But there are a host of other causes ranging from changes in raw material prices to exchange rates, wage settlements to government credit policies, the virtuosity of management to the ingenuity of the opposition, and from a capacity to plan to a will to implement.

What we have been arguing gives more substance to the notions of an uncertain or changing environment as propounded by Burns and Stalker or Lawrence and Lorsch. These phenomena of technical, market, and profitability change mean that firms can seldom stand still. The product which sells today may be a Luddite joke at the end of the decade, a market at present untapped may become saturated, today's business *démarche* may be tomorrow's sick joke. These are the reasons why companies have to think about the future, what it is going to do to them and what they are going to do back. The plans formulated as a result of these deliberations constitute corporate strategy, and strategic decisions are its constituent parts.

Thus a strategic decision is one which is concerned with the scope of an organisation's activities, rather than about how to do what it is doing already.[11] It is about where to draw the organisation's boundaries, what the organisation is going to do and be like. Strategy is about matching the organisation's activities to its environment, about plans requiring inputs the environment can supply and generating outputs the environment wants.

It follows that strategy is about matching the activities of a business to its resource capability. The business must, that is, be able to find or provide the resources to go with the plans, whether these resources are know-how, capital, management talent, or technical capacity. This means that strategic decisions will usually have major resource implications. They will have the effect of earmarking resources for this rather than that, or of generating needs for more resources to be deployed in particular ways and places.

It goes without saying that strategic decisions are intended to affect the long-term direction of a company. Strategic decisions cover big issues, and have a long time horizon. Examples include decisions to change the product range, to scrap established (but declining) products and develop new ones; to 'move sideways' and enter new industries; to attack new markets, face new competitors, try to sell abroad; to close plants, open new plants, establish a manufacturing facility abroad; to give up R&D, to make under licence, to pirate products, or to begin a new R&D initiative that will take 15 years to pay off.

Clearly strategic decisions are usually complex. They take account of considerations inside and outside the company, they have ramifications and implications. They are not just about quality control or sales methods or personnel policies.

If we stay with the textbook version for a moment the model for the development of corporate strategy goes something like this. First, strategic objectives will be set at a rather high level of generality, in terms of the scope of the business and the wished-for return on investment. Second, a strategic analysis is undertaken which scans the environment for developments which threaten the organisation or open up opportunities for it, and at the same time the organisation's resources are assessed, together with the likelihood of enlarging them. Third, top management generates strategic options, that is alternative plans for achieving the general objectives as at stage one. These options are then evaluated, the company 'firms up' on a particular strategy, and proceeds to its implementation, which in turn will involve allocating resources, perhaps making changes to the organisation structure in ways explored in the previous section, and establishing control systems to monitor the achievement of the strategic objectives.[12]

This is the model, and it does encapsulate what, from an analytical standpoint, is necessarily involved in corporate-strategy development. In practice there are often significant departures from the model. The most obvious departure is this: corporate strategy is like regular exercise, it is good for you, but this does not mean everyone does it. In short, many firms do not engage in corporate planning, or they do it too late or too skimpily. Generalising shamelessly, the companies which do engage in corporate strategy formulation tend to be the large, the technically sophisticated, the professionally managed, and the American owned.

There is, however, a more subtle mix of departures from the model. The essence of these is that the model implies a set of objectively rational procedures which are unlikely to be realised in practice. The act of corporate planning in reality will be less rational, and more idiosynchratic. It will reflect the prejudices and preferences of those doing it, and is likely to incorporate all sorts of biases, and intellectual short-circuits. Take for instance the 'generation of strategic options'. What real people conceive of as viable options will be heavily conditioned not only by their personal wishes but also by the corporate culture, traditions, pure chance, and the dynamics of political infighting (option b is never very attractive if it is advanced by the colleague you dislike most!). In short, the full range of options, rationally conceived, is unlikely to be reviewed in practice.

Corporate strategy represents an answer to the question: How do companies succeed? The answer is that they succeed in part by not standing still, by thinking intelligently and systematically about their operations and resources, the environment and its challenges, and what to go for in the future.

Corporate policy exists as an entity, and as a discipline. It has its own models and techniques, its professional practitioners, and a substantial theoretical and research literature. In all these senses it has developed in time side by side with the organisational theories of corporate success explored earlier in this chapter. Unlike them it posits action by real people, wilful and not necessarily rational, but acting to control the corporate future.

There is a final and recent strand of thinking about the success of companies, but first it will help to explore the underlying concept, corporate culture.

CORPORATE CULTURE

The idea of national cultures, and differences between them, was introduced in earlier discussions on the work and experiences of both export salesmen and managers sent to work abroad for their companies (chapters 6 and 7). This idea of culture has its counterpart at the level of the company itself, so that one may speak of corporate cultures, having common values and shared meanings as their essence.[13]

This notion of corporate culture is not so much the product of management research as an idea borrowed from anthropology. In particular the values common to members of a corporate culture, or the meanings these people share, should take account of two particular contingencies, the organisation's need for integration and its need to adapt to the environment. In other words the corporate culture should contain some loosely shared beliefs that legitimise whatever means the organisation has for keeping itself together and relating to its environment. As with national culture these beliefs, these shared meanings, do not have to be taken on board in any absolute way: they are just more or less accepted by most members most of the time.

How may these corporate cultures be analysed? In terms of what dimensions is it possible to plot corporate cultures? It has to be admitted that there is not any finite or comprehensive answer to these questions, yet one can still point to some recurrent dimensions in corporate cultures.

One can, for instance, characterise companies as sleepy or thrusting, production dominated or market led, egalitarian or hierarchic, as oriented to planning (corporate strategy) or merely reactive in the sense of having a fire-fighting orientation. To offer a strong example on the last-named dimension, that of planning to fire-fighting, the British pharmaceuticals company Fisons showed a massive commitment to strategic planning in the 1980s, one that involved a substantial element of divestment, of withdrawing from certain products and markets to develop others. Divestment on this scale requires resolution and a real belief in the planning exercise.

Sometimes one can point to elements of corporate culture which relate to and in part govern something quite specific. The Anglo-American accountancy practice Arthur Anderson, for example, has been stigmatised as a 'workaholic meritocracy' by some graduate recruits, which means this firm seeks to homogenise such recruits through a heavy reliance on in-house training and development. One of its rivals, however, manifests the opposite orientation by seeking to recruit very diverse people in the first place and then foster their heterogenity as an investment in future creativity.

The idea of corporate culture is important because these cultures may be functional or dysfunctional. The set of beliefs and shared meanings may, that is, broadly support and facilitate the aims of the company, or the reverse. Or it may be somewhere in the middle, or facilitate some aspects of company endeavour but not others.

The importance of a corporate culture may be more salient in connection with change. When a company tries to do something new, its success or failure in this endeavour may in no small way be determined by its culture. Suppose the company culture extols the virtues of reliability, stability, and tradition, and that this is wholly appropriate to its established business. Then, say, to compensate for a sagging market it enters a new arena, one calling for instant responses and 'fast footwork'. The corporate culture in the new case will be dysfunctional. The same situation may arise with take-overs, mergers, or acquisitions. An insurance company, say, feeling that its market must be nearing saturation point, takes over an oil-exploration company. Might this entail a mis-match of corporate cultures?

ENTER EXCELLENCE

A blockbuster of a book *In Search of Excellence* hit the bookshops late in 1982, the work of two American consultants, Peters and Waterman.[14] It made publishing history by selling a million copies in year one. If it has a simple message, it is that excellent companies achieve their success through the corporate culture rather than by means of strategy or structure.

Indeed their book starts out as an attack on structure and strategy:

> The Belgian Surrealist Rene Magritte painted a series of pipes and entitled the series *Ceci n'est pas une pipe* (This is not a pipe). The picture of the thing is not the thing. In the same way, an organisation chart is not a company, nor a new strategy an automatic answer to corporate grief.[15]

The authors do not so much object to stategy-structure *per se*, but to what they see as the excesses associated with them. These include an over reliance on strategy, exaggerated rationality, endless 'number-crunching' exercises in support of corporate-policy decisions and treating rational decision-making as the only consequential business activity. Instead Peters and Waterman opt for the importance of shared values, people, management skills and style.

The design of their study is breathtakingly simple (once someone has thought of it!). The authors first set up half a dozen financial performance criteria for business companies of the earnings per share and profit-to-sales-ratio kind. They then measure the performance of American companies in terms of these criteria over a 20-year period, from the 1960s to the 1980s. To qualify as 'excellent' an individual company must be on the top half of the scale for its industry, on at least four out of the six criteria, for the whole 20-year period. Having in this way generated a sample of excellent American companies by sustained and publicly verifiable performance Peters and Waterman then examine them, characterise them and indeed seek to say what is different and interesting about them. This main operation proceeds very much in terms of the 'soft' phenomena of style and culture rather than the hard phenomena of structure, strategy, and rational decision-making.

The result of this investigation is to say that eight attributes emerged, as the authors put it, 'to characterise most nearly the distinction of the excellent'.[16]

— *a bias for action*, a penchant for getting on with it; however rational their approach to decision-making the excellent companies are not paralysed by it; at the end of the day they will do something rather than nothing
— *close to the customer*; the excellent companies aim to learn from the people they serve, to be good on quality, reliability, and service and this marks them off
— *autonomy and entrepreneurship*; the excellent companies generate leaders and entrepreneurs throughout the organisation, people who have the will and the opportunity to be creative, and are not afraid of making mistakes
— *productivity through people*, in the sense that the excellent companies have an integrative not divisive view of labour, that they see production workers as the guarantee of quality and output gains
— *hands-on, value-driven*, in that the things these companies prize like quality and service are real working things, and the bosses will visibly line up in support of them
— *stick to the knitting*, or a sense of business craftsmanship; in practice this means that the excellent companies stick to the business they know, and avoid acquiring any business they don't know how to run
— *simple form, lean staff*; although all the excellent companies are big they are not top heavy, have simple structures, and keep the size of head-office staff within bounds
— *simultaneous loose-tight properties*, in that the excellent companies fiercely control a few things they hold to be really important, while decentralising in more general terms and allowing a lot of freedom to workers, junior managers, and product-development teams.

This in short form is the Peters and Waterman message. Its

power derives from its simplicity in no small way. There is a homely, folksy quality about much of it – stick to what you know, give your customers good service, give people freedom to create – yet every proposition is powerfully and persuasively argued in the original book with myriad examples from the successful companies.

In this it is a landmark in thinking about corporate success, as well as a reaction against the rationalist substructure of corporate strategy.

SYNTHESIS OR VISION?

There is time for a last idea. *In Search of Excellence* will probably never be superseded, but it has been followed by *Creating Excellence*.[17] This is the work of two more American consultants, Hickman and Silva.

Creating Excellence is based on yet another brilliantly simple idea (now that someone else has thought of it). This is that corporate excellence is produced by a judicious match of strategy *and* culture. The top manager or prime mover must be a strategic thinker and culture builder.

Take a simple example from Hickman and Silva, concerning Nolan Bushnell, the founder of Atari:

> Guided by a strategy bent on technological innovation and revaluation, Atari chalked up two shattering successes – arcade and then home versions of an electronic ping-pong game called Pong. By 1975, sales blasted to $39 million, net income to $3.5 million. In three short years Bushnell had build a forceful culture at Atari committed to innovation and fun. Creative, game-loving engineers set the pace, management allowed people to come to work in T-shirts at any hour they chose (as long as the ideas and innovations kept flowing), and workers at all levels engaged in marathon brainstorming sessions.[18]

The idea of strategy plus culture is elegant and appealing. Hickman and Silva make a start on the problem of unpacking it and illustrating it, but this is just a start. The formula generates two key questions which require a systematic answer, and one which takes account of the different circumstances of industries. The questions, which overlap, are: What will it look like in practice, and how do you do it?

NOTES

1 A very vigorous presentation of the case for decentralisation in the form of divisionalisation, breaking down a big company into independent operating divisions, is developed by America's most famous and prolific management writer on the basis of his consultancy study of General Motors: Peter Drucker (1946) *The Concept of the Corporation*, John Day Company, New York.

2 This technology-structure study appears in Joan Woodward (1965) *Industrial Organisation: Theory and Practice*, Oxford University Press, London.

3 For a summary of the Joan Woodward thesis, with engaging diagrams, see Peter Lawrence and Robert Lee (1984) *Insight into Management*, Oxford University Press, London, chapter 2.

4 This second British study which works from the Battle of Britain to a theory relating organisational structure to corporate success is: T. Burns and G. M. Stalker (1961) *The Management of Innovation*, Tavistock Publications, London.

5 Again a more detailed account of the Burns and Stalker's mechanistic and organic structures, with diagrams, is offered in: Lawrence and Lee, op. cit.

6 P. R. Lawrence and J. W. Lorsch (1967) *Organisation and Environment*, Harvard University Press, Cambridge, Mass.

7 For a good discussion of the various specialisms making up the personnel function see Paul Windolf (1985) Personnel management: an organisational perspective, in Peter Lawrence and Ken Elliott (eds) *Introducing Management*, Penguin, Harmondsworth, Middlesex.

8 These linked questions of genuine differences of interest between functions or departments and the difficulties of higher managers charged with integrating them are

explored in more detail in Peter Lawrence (1984) *Management in Action*, Routledge & Kegan Paul, London, chapter 3.

9 A more scholarly and sophisticated version of the argument developed in this section is offered by John Child (1973) Organisational structure, environment and performance: the role of strategic choice, in Graeme Salaman and Kenneth Thompson (eds) *People and Organisations*, Longman, London.

10 This discussion of corporate strategy draws heavily on Jerry Johnson (1985) Corporate strategy and strategic management, in Peter Lawrence and Ken Elliott (eds) *Introducing Management*, Penguin, Harmondsworth, Middlesex.

11 Ibid.

12 Ibid.

13 For a more detailed account of corporate culture see Robert Lee and Peter Lawrence (1985) *Organisational Behaviour: Politics at Work*, Hutchinson, London, chapter 5.

14 Thomas J. Peters and Robert H. Waterman Jr. (1982) *In Search of Excellence*, Harper & Row, New York.

15 Ibid., p. 3.

16 Ibid., p. 13.

17 Craig R. Hickman and Michael A. Silva (1984) *Creating Excellence*, Allen & Unwin, London.

18 Ibid., p. 80.

Further Reading

In these further-reading suggestions I will try to do two things. First and most obviously these suggestions will take further themes explored in the book. I have tried to write about what management is and what management does and most of the further-reading ideas build on this and are sources that have been cited in the notes to individual chapters. The second thing is to say that although this book has not been about all the taught specialisms that make up courses in management, overviewed in chapter 1, I offer a few suggestions for further reading along these lines to redress the balance a little.

Daniel Boorstin's social and cultural history of the USA does not have much to do with management in any direct sense, but it is so good it deserves to be recommended to anyone who is interested in what societies are like and how they change! It is Daniel J. Boorstin (1969) *The Americans: the National Experience*, Penguin Books, Harmondsworth, Middlesex.

The two classics on the theme of 'what managers do all day' are: Sune Carlson (1951) *Executive Behaviour*, Strombergs, Stockholm, and Henry Minztberg (1973) *The Nature of Managerial Work*, Harper & Row, New York. Another work in the same tradition but oriented to production managers rather than chief executives is Peter Lawrence (1984) *Management in Action*, Routledge & Kegan Paul, London.

A more detailed account of the various functions of management – sales, personnel, production, and so on – is to be found in both Peter Lawrence and Robert Lee (1984) *Insight into Management*, Oxford University Press, London, and in Peter Lawrence and Ken Elliott (eds) (1985) *Introducing Management*, Penguin, Harmondsworth, Middlesex. On the systematic analysis of the differences between management jobs, and the choices facing the manager, Rosemary Stewart is the authority and her three books (1964) *Managers and their Jobs*, Pan, London, (1976) *Contrasts in Management*, McGraw Hill, Maidenhead, Berkshire, and (1982) *Choices for the Manager*, McGraw Hill, Maidenhead, Berkshire, are all strongly recommended.

On the subject of the process of management there are two musts. In my view the book by Leonard R. Sayles (1979) *Leadership: What Effective Managers Really Do and How They Do It*, McGraw Hill Book Company, New York, is in a class of its own, and Melvil Dalton (1959) *Men Who Manage*, John Wiley, New York, is a classic of the management underworld.

Together with colleagues at Loughborough University I have written a book on small firms: Peter Lawrence (ed) (1985) *Small Business Breakthrough*, Basil Blackwell, Oxford, and it contains a good bibliography on small firms in Europe and the USA.

There is an excellent book on buying and selling in Europe comparing the performance of several countries including Britain: Peter Turnbull and Malcolm Cunningham (1981) *International Marketing and Purchasing*, Macmillan, London. On the question of work-related cultural differences between countries the classic is: Geert Hofstede (1980) *Cultures Consequences*, Sage Publications, Beverley Hills/London. For the other side of the picture, the view that industrial countries are becoming increasingly alike, see: Clark Kerr *et al*. (1960) *Industrialism and Industrial Man*, Harvard University Press, Cambridge, Mass.

On individual managers, their motives and successes these books in particular deserve to be strongly recommended. First Alan Bryman has brought together the vast literature on leadership in (1986) *Leadership and Organisations*, Routledge & Kegan Paul, London. Second Michael Maccoby (1978) *The Gamesman*, Bantam Books, New York, is a very readable and insightful look at what drives managers to success. Lastly John Kotter (1982) *The General Managers*, The Free Press, New York, is very good both on the reality of top management work and on the determinants of individual career success.

On the success of companies the outstanding and very readable book is Thomas J. Peters and Robert H. Waterman Jr. (1982) *In Search of Excellence*, Harper & Row, New York. There is a British sequl, not as striking but still well worth reading, Walter Goldsmith and David Clutterbuck (1984) *The Winning Streak*, Weidenfeld & Nicolson, London. My own view is that the book which takes these arguments further, Craig R. Hickman and Michael A. Silva (1984) *Creating Excellence*, Allen & Unwin, London, will come to serve as the beginning of a new genre.

Moving next to the management specialisms as taught on higher education courses, on production management textbooks the established classic is Keith Locker (1984) *Production Management*, 4th edn, Pitman, London, and the relative and very good newcomer is: Terry Hill (1984) *Production/Operations Management*, Prentice Hall, London.

On the quantitative analysis side a good recent operations research text is David Johnson (1986) *Quantitative Business Analysis*, Butterworth, London; and on mathematical modelling, Paul Finlay (1985) *Mathematical Modelling in Business Decision-Making*, Croom Helm, London, breaks new ground.

John Sizer (1979) *An Insight into Management Accounting*, 2nd edn, Penguin, Harmondsworth, Middlesex, is about how management accounting is used inside the firm, and John Blake (1985) *Financial Accounting: An Introduction*, Hutchinson, London, looks at the conventions which underlie accounting information and how it can serve the needs of a wide range of users.

Of the several introductory books on marketing I am inclined to go for: T. Cannon (1980) *Basic Marketing*, Holt Rinehart & Winston, Eastbourne, Sussex. Jerry Johnson and Kevin Scholes (1984) *Exploring Corporate Strategy*, Prentice Hall, London, is an excellent text on business policy/corporate strategy.

Robert Lee and Peter Lawrence (1985) *Organisational Behaviour: Politics at Work*, Hutchinson, London, summarises a lot of the organisational behaviour literature and gives it a new look.

Finally I have lived, at least for short periods, in several countries besides Britain. In management terms I know West Germany well, and Sweden quite well, and I have drawn on both in writing this book. For any reader who is interested in either of these countries more rounded accounts are to be found in: Peter Lawrence (1980) *Managers and Management in West Germany*, Croom Helm, London, and Peter Lawrence and Tony Spybey (1986) *Management and Society in Sweden*, Routledge & Kegan Paul, London.

Index